United States Government Accoun

GAO

By the Comptroller Ge
United States

September 2013

STANDARDS FOR INTERNAL CONTROL IN THE FEDERAL GOVERNMENT

2013 Exposure Draft

GAO-13-830SP

GAO

U.S. GOVERNMENT ACCOUNTABILITY OFFICE

441 G St. N.W.
Washington, DC 20548

September 2013

To Federal Officials and Others Interested in *Standards for Internal Control in the Federal Government*

GAO invites your comments on the accompanying proposed changes to *Standards for Internal Control in the Federal Government*, commonly known as the "Green Book." This letter describes the process used by GAO for revising the Green Book, summarizes the proposed major changes, discusses proposed effective dates, and provides instructions for submitting comments on the proposed standards.

Process for Revising the Green Book

To help ensure that the standards continue to meet the needs of the federal community and the public it serves, the Comptroller General of the United States established the Advisory Council on Standards for Internal Control in the Federal Government (Green Book Advisory Council) to review GAO's revision of the standards and consider any other necessary changes. The Green Book Advisory Council includes experts in financial management drawn from federal, state, and local government; the private sector; public accounting; and academia. This exposure draft includes the Green Book Advisory Council's input regarding the proposed changes. We are currently requesting public comments on the proposed revisions in the exposure draft.

Summary of Major Changes

The proposed revision to the Green Book will be the third since GAO first issued the standards in 1983. The proposed changes contained in the 2013 Exposure Draft update the Green Book to reflect major developments in the accountability and financial management profession and emphasize specific considerations applicable to the government environment.

Enclosure I to this letter contains a discussion of the major changes.

Effective Dates

When issued in final form, this revision will supersede the November 1999 revision of the standards. The effective date for this revision, as well as transition guidance to help officials implement the revised standards, will be included when the Green Book is issued in final form.

Instructions for Commenting

The draft of the proposed changes to *Standards for Internal Control in the Federal Government*, 2013 Exposure Draft, is only available in electronic format and can be downloaded from GAO's Green Book web page at: http://www.gao.gov/greenbook.

- - - - -

We are requesting comments on this draft from federal officials; managers and auditors at all levels of government; the public accounting profession; academia; professional organizations; public interest groups; and other interested parties. To assist you in developing your comments, specific issues are presented in enclosure II to this letter. We encourage you to comment on these issues and any additional issues that you note. Please associate your comments with specific references to question numbers in the enclosure and/or paragraph numbers in the proposed standards and provide your rationale for any suggested changes, along with suggested revised language. All comments received from the public will be considered a matter of public record and will ultimately be posted on the GAO website.

Please send your comment letters to our Green Book inbox: GreenBook@gao.gov no later than December 2, 2013.

If you need additional information please contact me at (202) 512-3133 or dalkinj@gao.gov.

James Dalkin
Director, Financial Management and Assurance

Enclosures - 2

Enclosure I: Summary of Major Changes

The 2013 revision of the *Standards for Internal Control in the Federal Government* represents a modernized version of the standards. These standards take into account the developments made in government in the area of internal control. These standards provide management criteria for designing, implementing, and operating an internal control system and reinforce management's accountability for internal control.

This revision does not change the previous standards on a conceptual level. The revised standards retain the five components of internal control, but introduce 17 principles to assist management in achieving an effective internal control system. These principles were adopted from the Committee of Sponsoring Organizations of the Treadway Commission's revision of its *Internal Control: Integrated Framework* and adapted for the government environment. The revised standards also introduce attributes that support these principles and further define the requirements for an effective internal control system.

Enclosure II: Questions for Commenters

The following questions are provided to guide users in commenting on the 2013 Exposure Draft of the *Standards for Internal Control in the Federal Government*. We encourage you to comment on these issues and any additional issues that you note. Please associate your comments with specific references to question numbers, paragraph numbers, or both in the proposed standards and provide your rationale for any proposed changes, along with suggested revised language.

1. Is the hierarchy of components, principles, and attributes clearly explained?

2. Are there any internal control concepts unique to the government environment that should be in the Green Book that are not currently included?

3. Does the framework provide the necessary information to allow program managers to evaluate the internal controls for their programs?

4. Does the Green Book provide adequate criteria for auditors?

5. Are the requirements for management to design, implement, and operate an internal control system clear, understandable, and adequate?

6. Is the evaluation of deficiencies discussion clear, understandable, and adequate?

7. Are the roles, divisions, and overlaps of responsibility for the oversight body, management, and personnel clear, understandable, and adequate?

8. Are the documentation requirements included in the Green Book clear, understandable, and adequate?

9. Is there a need for additional internal control implementation guidance? If so, what form should it take?

10. Is this Green Book written in such a way to allow state, local, and quasi-governmental entities, as well as not-for-profit organizations, to adapt it for their own use?

Contents

Overview

Foreword

Policymakers and program managers are continually seeking ways to improve accountability in achieving an entity's mission. A key factor in improving accountability in achieving an entity's mission is to implement an effective internal control system. An effective internal control system helps an entity adapt to shifting environments, evolving demands, and new priorities. As programs change and entities strive to improve operational processes and implement new technology, management continually evaluates its internal control system to ensure that it is effective and updated when necessary.

Section 3512 (c) and (d) of Title 31 of the United States Code (commonly known as the Federal Managers' Financial Integrity Act (FMFIA)) requires the Comptroller General to issue standards for internal control in government. These standards, known as the *Standards for Internal Control in the Federal Government* (Green Book), provide the overall framework for establishing and maintaining an effective internal control system. Office of Management and Budget (OMB) Circular No. A-123, *Management's Responsibility for Internal Control*, provides specific requirements for assessing and reporting on controls in the federal government. The term "internal control" in this document covers all aspects of an entity's objectives (operations, reporting, and compliance).

The Green Book may also be applied by state, local, and quasi-governmental entities, as well as not-for-profit organizations, as a framework for an internal control system. Management of these entities determines, based on applicable laws and regulations, how to appropriately adapt the framework presented in the Green Book for an entity.

The Committee of Sponsoring Organizations of the Treadway Commission (COSO) updated its internal control guidance in 2013 with the issuance of a revised *Internal Control - Integrated Framework*.[1] COSO has introduced the concept of principles related to the five components of internal control.

---

[1] See Committee of Sponsoring Organizations of the Treadway Commission (COSO) *Internal Control – Integrated Framework* (May 2013)

We have adapted these principles in developing this update. When finalized, the updated Green Book will supersede those previously issued.[2]

---

[2] See GAO *Standards for Internal Control in the Federal Government,* GAO/AIMD-00-21.3.1 (Washington, D.C.: November 1999)

How to Use the Green Book

We are issuing the Green Book to provide managers with internal control criteria to help them design, implement, and operate an effective internal control system. Our goal is to define the standards of internal control through the components, principles, and relevant attributes of internal control and explain why they are integral to an entity's internal control system. We recognize that in discussing internal control, we are separating internal control from the operational processes in which it occurs. We have done so to clarify what processes management considers part of internal control. In a mature and highly effective internal control system, internal control may be indistinguishable from day-to-day activities personnel perform.

We have structured the Green Book as follows:

1. An overview, including:

- Section 1: an overview of the fundamental concepts of internal control

- Section 2: a discussion of internal control components, principles, and attributes; how these relate to an entity's objectives; and the three categories of objectives

- Section 3: a discussion of how management evaluates the internal control system's design, implementation, and operation

- Section 4: additional considerations that apply to all components in an internal control system

2. A discussion of the requirements for each of the five components, 17 principles, and related attributes as well as additional discussion of the requirements

We have clearly marked the requirements for the Green Book through the use of "must" and "should." For further discussion of the requirements, please refer to sections 2 and 3 of the Overview.

Section 1 - Fundamental Concepts of Internal Control

Definition of Internal Control

O1.01 Internal control is an integral component of an entity's management that provides reasonable assurance that the objectives of an entity are being achieved. These objectives and related risks can be broadly classified into one or more of the three following categories:

- Operations - Effectiveness and efficiency of operations

- Reporting - Reliability of reporting for internal and external use

- Compliance - Compliance with applicable laws and regulations

O1.02 These are distinct but overlapping categories. A particular objective can fall under more than one category, can address different needs, and may be the direct responsibility of different individuals.

O1.03 Internal control comprises the plans, methods, policies, and procedures used to fulfill the mission, strategic plan, goals, and objectives of the organization. Internal control serves as the first line of defense in safeguarding assets. In short, internal control helps federal managers achieve desired results through effective stewardship of public resources.

An Internal Control System

O1.04 An internal control system is a continuous built-in component of operations, effected by people, that provides reasonable assurance, not absolute assurance, that an organization's objectives will be achieved.

O1.05 Internal control is not one event, but a series of actions that occur throughout an entity's operations. Internal control is recognized as an integral part of the operational processes management uses to regulate and guide its operations rather than as a separate system within an entity. In this sense, internal control is built into the entity as a part of the organizational structure to help managers achieve the entity's objectives on an ongoing basis.

O1.06 People are what make internal control work. Management is responsible for an effective internal control system. As part of this responsibility, management sets the entity's objectives, implements controls, and evaluates the internal control system. However, personnel throughout an organization play important roles in implementing and operating an effective internal control system.

O1.07 An effective internal control system increases the likelihood that an entity will achieve its objectives. However, no matter how well designed, implemented, or operated, an internal control system cannot provide absolute assurance that all of an organization's objectives will be met. Factors outside the control or influence of management can affect the entity's ability to achieve all of its objectives. For example, a natural disaster can affect an organization's ability to achieve its objectives. Therefore, once in place, effective internal control provides reasonable, not absolute, assurance that an organization will achieve its objectives.

Section 2 - Establishing an Effective Internal Control System

Presentation of Standards

O2.01 The Green Book defines the standards for internal control in the federal government. FMFIA requires federal executive branch entities to establish internal control in accordance with these standards. The standards provide criteria for assessing the design, implementation, and operating effectiveness of internal control in federal government entities to determine if an internal control system is effective. An entity must have an effective internal control system to comply with the standards.

O2.02 The Green Book applies to all aspects of an entity's objectives: operations, reporting, and compliance. However, these standards are not intended to limit or interfere with duly granted authority related to legislation, rule-making, or other discretionary policy-making in an organization. In implementing the Green Book, management is responsible for designing the policies and procedures to fit an entity's operations and building them in as an integral part of the entity's operations.

Components, Principles, and Attributes

O2.03 An entity determines its mission, sets a strategic plan, establishes entity objectives, and formulates plans to achieve its objectives. Management, with oversight from the entity's oversight body, may set objectives for an entity as a whole, or target activities within the entity.

Management uses internal control to help the organization achieve these objectives. While there are different ways to present internal control, the Green Book approaches internal control through a hierarchical structure of five components, 17 principles, and relevant attributes.

O2.04 The five components of internal control are:

- Control Environment - The foundation for an internal control system. It provides the discipline and structure to help an entity achieve its objectives.

- Risk Assessment - Assesses the risks facing the entity as it seeks to achieve its objectives. This assessment provides the basis for developing appropriate risk responses.

- Control Activities - The actions management establishes through policies and procedures to achieve objectives and respond to risks in the internal control system, which includes the entity's information system.

- Information and Communication - The quality information management uses to support the internal control system. Communicating quality information is vital for an entity to run and control its operations.

- Monitoring - Assesses the quality of performance over time and ensures that the findings of audits and other reviews are promptly resolved.

O2.05 These five components represent the highest level of the hierarchy of standards for internal control in the federal government. The principles and underlying attributes represent the requirements necessary to achieve the standards of internal control. In the Green Book, these requirements are identified through use of specific language. The Green Book uses the word "should" to denote a principle or attribute statement.

O2.06 In general, all components, principles, and attributes are relevant for an effective internal control system. However, there may be an operating or regulatory situation in which management has determined that a principle or attribute is not relevant for the entity to achieve its objectives and address related risks. Relevance refers to management's determination that each principle and attribute has a significant bearing on the design, implementation, and operation of its associated component. If management decides a principle or attribute is not relevant, management supports that determination with documentation that includes the rationale of how, in the absence of that principle or attribute, the associated component could be designed, implemented, and operated effectively.

O2.07 In addition to principle and attribute requirements, the Green Book contains additional information in the form of application material. Application material provides further explanation of the principle and attribute requirements and may explain more precisely what a requirement means and what it is intended to cover, or include examples of procedures that may be appropriate for an entity. The words "may," "might," and "could" are used to describe these procedures. The application material may also provide background information on matters addressed in the Green Book. Although application material does not impose a requirement, it is relevant to the proper implementation of the requirements. Management has a responsibility to understand the application material and exercise judgment in fulfilling the requirements of the principles and attributes.

O2.08 Management has a responsibility to consider the entire text of the Green Book in designing, implementing, and operating an internal control system. The Green Book, however, does not prescribe the process for how management designs, implements, and operates its internal control system.

O2.09 Below are the five components of internal control and 17 related principles. The related attributes are covered in the respective component chapters.

Control environment	Control activities
1. The oversight body and management should demonstrate a commitment to integrity and ethical values.	**10.** Management should design control activities to achieve objectives and risk responses.
2. The oversight body should oversee the entity's internal control system.	**11.** Management should design control activities for the entity's information system.
3. Management should establish an organizational structure, assign responsibility, and delegate authority to achieve the entity's objectives.	**12.** Management should implement control activities.
	Information and communication
4. Management should demonstrate a commitment to attract, develop, and retain competent individuals.	**13.** Management should use quality information.
5. Management should evaluate performance and hold individuals accountable for their internal control responsibilities.	**14.** Management should internally communicate the necessary quality information.
Risk assessment	**15.** Management should externally communicate the necessary quality information.
6. Management should define objectives and risk tolerances.	**Monitoring**
7. Management should identify, analyze, and respond to risks related to achieving the defined objectives.	**16.** Management should establish monitoring activities to monitor the internal control system and evaluate the results.
8. Management should consider the potential for fraud when identifying, analyzing, and responding to risks.	**17.** Management should ensure identified internal control deficiencies are remediated on a timely basis.
9. Management should identify, analyze, and respond to significant changes in the internal control system.	

Source: GAO.

Internal Control and the Entity

O2.10 A direct relationship exists among an entity's objectives, the five components of internal control, and the organizational structure of an entity. Objectives are what an entity wants to achieve. The five components of internal control are what is required of the entity to achieve the objectives. Organizational structure encompasses the operating units, operational processes, and other structures management uses to achieve the objectives. This relationship is depicted in the form of a cube developed by COSO.[3]

---

[3] See paras. 3.03 through 3.07 for further discussion of organizational structure.

GAO 13-830SP Green Book Exposure Draft

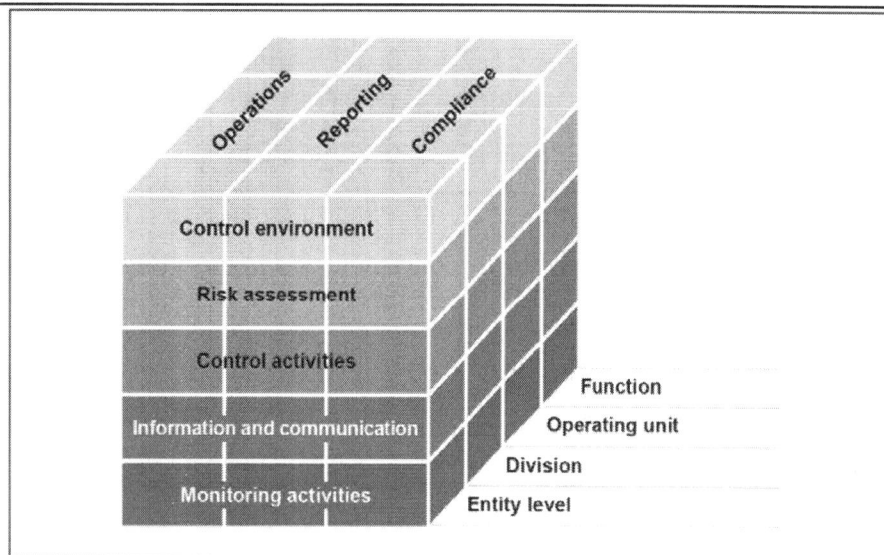

Source: COSO.

O2.11 The three categories into which an entity's objectives can be classified are represented by the columns labelled on top of the cube. The five components of internal control are represented by the rows. The organizational structure is represented by the third dimension of the cube.

O2.12 Each component of internal control applies to all three categories of objectives and the organizational structure.

O2.13 Internal control is a dynamic, iterative, and integrated process in which components impact the design, implementation, and operating effectiveness of each other. No two entities will have an identical internal control system due to differences in factors such as mission, regulatory environment, strategic plan, entity size, risk tolerance, and information technology.

Roles in an Internal Control System

O2.14 Because internal control is a part of management's overall responsibility, the five components are discussed in the context of the management of the entity. However, everyone in the organization has a responsibility for internal control. In general, roles in an entity's internal control system can be categorized as follows:

- Oversight body - The oversight body is responsible for overseeing the strategic direction of the entity and obligations related to the

GAO 13-830SP Green Book Exposure Draft

accountability of the entity. This includes overseeing management's design, implementation, and operation of an internal control system. For some entities, an oversight body might be one or a few members of senior management. For other entities, multiple parties may be members of the entity's oversight body. For the purpose of the Green Book, oversight by an oversight body is implicit in each principle and attribute.

- Management - Management is directly responsible for all activities of an organization, including the design, implementation, and operating effectiveness of an entity's internal control system. Managers' responsibilities vary depending on their functions in the organizational structure.

- Personnel - Personnel help management design, implement, and operate an internal control system and are responsible for reporting issues noted in the entity's operations, compliance, or reporting objectives.[4]

O2.15 External auditors and the Office of Inspector General (IG) are not considered a part of an entity's internal control system. While management may evaluate and incorporate recommendations by external auditors and the IG, responsibility for an entity's internal control system resides with management.

Objectives of an Entity

O2.16 Management, with oversight by an oversight body, sets objectives to meet the entity's mission, requirements of applicable laws and regulations, strategic plan, and goals. Management sets objectives before designing an entity's internal control system. Management may include setting objectives as part of the strategic planning process.

O2.17 Management, as part of designing an internal control system, defines the objectives in specific and measureable terms to enable management to identify, analyze, and respond to risks related to achieving those objectives.

Categories of Objectives
O2.18 Management groups objectives into one or more of the three categories of objectives:

---

[4] See paras. 16.01 through 17.10 for further discussion on identifying issues.

- Operations - Effectiveness and efficiency of operations
- Reporting - Reliability of reporting for internal and external use
- Compliance - Compliance with applicable laws and regulations

Operations Objectives

O2.19 Operations objectives relate to program operations that achieve an entity's mission. An entity's mission may be defined in a strategic plan. Such plans set the goals and objectives for an entity along with the effective and efficient operations necessary to fulfill those objectives. Effective operations produce the intended results from operational processes while efficient operations do so in a manner that minimizes the waste of resources.

O2.20 Management can set, from the objectives, related subobjectives for units within the organizational structure. Management, by linking objectives throughout the entity to the mission, improves the effectiveness and efficiency of program operations in achieving the mission.

Reporting Objectives

O2.21 Reporting objectives relate to the preparation of reports for use by the entity, its stakeholders, or other external parties. Reporting objectives may be grouped further into subcategories:

- External Financial Reporting Objectives - Objectives related to the release of the entity's financial performance in accordance with professional standards, applicable laws and regulations, as well as expectations of stakeholders.

- External Nonfinancial Reporting Objectives - Objectives related to the release of nonfinancial information in accordance with professional standards, applicable laws and regulations, as well as expectations of stakeholders.

- Internal Financial Reporting Objectives and Nonfinancial Reporting Objectives - Objectives related to gathering information needed by management to support decision making and evaluation of the entity's performance.

Compliance Objectives

O2.22 In the government sector, objectives related to compliance with applicable laws and regulations can be more significant than in the private sector. Laws and regulations often prescribe a government entity's objectives, structure, methods to achieve objectives, and reporting of performance relative to achieving objectives. Management considers objectives in the category of compliance comprehensively for the entity and determines what controls would be necessary to design, implement, and operate for the entity to achieve these objectives effectively.

O2.23 Management conducts activities in accordance with applicable laws and regulations. As part of specifying compliance objectives, the entity determines which laws and regulations apply to the entity. Management is expected to set objectives that incorporate these requirements. Some entities may set objectives to a higher level of performance than established by laws and regulations. In setting those objectives, management is able to exercise discretion relative to the performance of the entity.

Safeguarding of Assets

O2.24 A subset of the three categories of objectives is the safeguarding of assets. Management designs an internal control system to provide reasonable assurance regarding prevention or prompt detection of unauthorized acquisition, use, or disposition of an entity's assets.

Setting Subobjectives

O2.25 Management can develop from objectives more specific subobjectives throughout the organizational structure. Management needs to define subobjectives in specific and measurable terms that can be communicated to the personnel who are assigned responsibility to achieve these subobjectives. Both management and personnel require an understanding of an objective, its subobjectives, and defined levels of performance to ensure accountability in an internal control system.

Section 3 - Evaluation of an Effective Internal Control System

Requirements for Effective Internal Control

O3.01 An effective internal control system provides reasonable assurance that the organization will achieve its objectives. It requires that

- each of the five components, 17 principles, and relevant attributes of internal control are effectively designed, implemented, and operating and

- the five components are operating together in an integrated manner.

O3.02 To determine if an internal control system meets these requirements, management evaluates the effect of internal control deficiencies on the internal control system.

Evaluation of Deficiencies in Internal Control

O3.03 Management evaluates control deficiencies identified by management's ongoing monitoring of the internal control system as well as any separate evaluations performed by both internal and external sources. A deficiency in internal control exists when the design, implementation, or operation of a control does not allow management or personnel, in the normal course of performing their assigned functions, to achieve control objectives and address related risks.

O3.04 In the federal government FMFIA mandates that the head of each executive agency annually prepare a statement as to whether the agency's systems of internal accounting and administrative controls comply with the requirements of the act. If the systems do not comply, the head of the agency will include a report in which any material weaknesses in the agency's system of internal accounting and administrative control are identified and the plans and schedule for correcting any such weakness are described.

Design and Implementation

O3.05 When evaluating design of internal control, management determines if controls individually and in combination with other controls are capable of achieving an objective and addressing related risks. When evaluating implementation, management determines if the control exists

13

and if the entity has placed the control into operation. A control cannot be effectively implemented if it was not effectively designed. A deficiency in design exists when (a) a control necessary to meet a control objective is missing or (b) an existing control is not properly designed so that even if the control operates as designed, the control objective would not be met. A deficiency in implementation exists when a properly designed control is not implemented correctly in the internal control system.

Operation

O3.06 In evaluating operating effectiveness, management determines if controls were applied at relevant times during the period under evaluation, the consistency with which they were applied, and by whom or by what means they were applied. If substantially different controls were used at different times during the period under evaluation, management evaluates operating effectiveness separately for each unique control system. A control cannot be effectively operating if it was not effectively designed and implemented. A deficiency in operation exists when a properly designed control does not operate as designed, or when the person performing the control does not possess the necessary authority or competence to perform the control effectively.

Effect on the Internal Control System

O3.07 Management evaluates the significance of identified deficiencies. Significance refers to the relative importance of a deficiency in the entity achieving a defined objective. To evaluate the significance of the deficiency, management assesses its effect on achieving the defined objectives at both the entity and transaction level. Management evaluates the significance of a deficiency by considering the magnitude of impact, likelihood of occurrence, and nature of the deficiency. Magnitude of impact refers to the likely effect that the deficiency could have on the entity achieving its objectives and is affected by factors such as the size, pace, and duration of the deficiency's impact. A deficiency may be more significant to one objective than another. Likelihood of occurrence refers to the possibility of a deficiency impacting an entity's ability to achieve its objectives. The nature of the deficiency involves factors such as the degree of subjectivity involved with the deficiency and whether the deficiency arises from fraud or misconduct. The oversight body oversees management's evaluation of significance of deficiencies to ensure that deficiencies have been properly considered.

O3.08 Deficiencies are evaluated both on an individual basis and in the aggregate. Management considers the correlation among different deficiencies or groups of deficiencies when evaluating their significance. Deficiency evaluation varies by entity because of differences in entities' objectives.

O3.09 Generally, management first considers whether controls are designed, implemented, and operating effectively to achieve each relevant attribute. The Green Book describes each attribute in general terms. For each attribute, management considers the elements underlying the attribute and whether controls are properly designed, implemented, and operating effectively to achieve each element of the attribute. If one or more of the elements are not achieved, then a deficiency in internal control exists. In determining whether an attribute is achieved, management considers whether the design, implementation, and operation of the controls, in the aggregate, are sufficient to fully achieve the attribute. Such consideration includes an assessment of the impact of identified deficiencies on the achievement of the attribute.

O3.10 For each principle, management makes a summary determination as to whether the principle is designed, implemented, and operating effectively by considering whether the related attributes are achieved. If a principle is not designed, implemented, or operating effectively, then the respective component is not likely to be effective, and an internal control system is unlikely to be effective in helping the entity in achieving its objectives.

O3.11 Based on the results of this evaluation, management then evaluates the design, implementation, and operating effectiveness of each of the five components of internal control and whether they operate together effectively. If one or more of the five components are not effectively designed, implemented, or operating effectively, then an internal control system is ineffective. Judgment is used in making such determinations, which includes exercising reasonable care.

Section 4 - Additional Considerations

Service Organizations

O4.01 Management may engage external parties to perform certain operational processes for the entity, such as accounting and payroll processing, security services, or healthcare claims processing. For the purpose of the Green Book, these external parties are referred to as "service organizations." Management, however, retains responsibility for the performance of processes assigned to service organizations. Therefore, management needs to understand the controls each service organization has designed, has implemented, and operates for the assigned operational process and how the service organization's internal control system impacts the entity's internal control system.

O4.02 Management also considers the complementary entity user controls identified by the service organization or its auditors. Management determines whether established internal controls are sufficient to ensure the entity achieves objectives and addresses risks related to the outsourced process or to incorporate the complementary user entity controls into the entity's internal control system.

O4.03 Management may consider the following when determining the extent of oversight controls for the service organization:

- The nature of services outsourced

- The service organization's standards of conduct

- Quality and frequency of the service organization's enforcement of adherence to standards of conduct by its personnel

- Magnitude and level of complexity of the entity's operations and organizational structure

Large versus Small Entities

O4.04 The 17 principles apply to both large and small entities. However, smaller entities may have different implementation approaches than larger entities. Smaller entities typically have unique advantages, which can contribute to an effective internal control system. These may include a higher level of involvement by management in operational processes and direct interaction with personnel. Smaller entities may find informal staff meetings effective for communicating quality information, where larger entities may need more formal mechanisms, such as written reports, intranet portals, or periodic formal meetings, to communicate with the organization.

O4.05 A smaller entity, however, faces greater challenges in segregating duties because of its concentration of responsibilities and authorities in the organizational structure.[5] Management, however, can respond to this increased risk through the design of the internal control system, such as by adding additional levels of review for key operational processes, reviewing randomly selected transactions and their supporting documentation, taking periodic asset counts, or checking supervisor reconciliations.

Benefits and Costs of Internal Control

O4.06 Internal control provides many benefits to an entity. It provides management with added confidence regarding the achievement of objectives, provides feedback on how effectively an entity is operating, and helps reduce risks related to achieving the entity's objectives. Management considers a variety of cost factors in relation to expected benefits when designing and implementing internal controls. The complexity of cost-benefit determination is compounded by the interrelationship of controls with operational processes. Where controls are integrated with operational processes, it is difficult to isolate either their costs or benefits.

O4.07 Management may decide how an entity evaluates the costs versus benefits of various approaches to implementing an effective internal control system. However, cost alone is not an acceptable reason to avoid implementing internal controls. Management is responsible for meeting internal control objectives. The cost versus benefits considerations support management's ability to design, implement, and operate effectively an internal control system that balances the allocation of human resources in relation to the areas of greatest risk, complexity, or other factors relevant to achieving the entity's objectives.

Documentation

O4.08 The Green Book has specified documentation requirements in five attributes in the framework, with discussion of these requirements in the accompanying application material. These are:

- Principle 3: Paragraph 3.12

- Principle 12: Paragraph 12.03

---

[5] See paras. 10.15 through 10.18 for further discussion of segregation of duties.

- Principle 16: Paragraph 16.12
- Principle 17: Paragraph 17.07
- Principle 17: Paragraph 17.09

O4.09 These attributes represent the minimum level of required documentation in an entity's internal control system. Management exercises judgment in determining what additional documentation may be required beyond these attributes for an effective internal control system.

Applicability to Other Entities

O4.10 The Green Book may be applied as a framework for an internal control system for state, local, and quasi-governmental entities, as well as not-for-profit organizations. Management of these entities determines, based on applicable laws and regulations, the applicable requirements for their entities. If management elects to use the Green Book as criteria, management follows all applicable requirements presented in these standards.

Control Environment

Overview

The control environment is the foundation for an internal control system. It provides the discipline and structure, which affect the overall quality of internal control. It influences how objectives are defined and how control activities are structured. The oversight body and management establish and maintain an environment throughout the organization that sets a positive attitude toward internal control.

Principles

1. The oversight body and management should demonstrate a commitment to integrity and ethical values.

2. The oversight body should oversee the entity's internal control system.

3. Management should establish an organizational structure, assign responsibility, and delegate authority to achieve the entity's objectives.

4. Management should demonstrate a commitment to attract, develop, and retain competent individuals.

5. Management should evaluate performance and hold individuals accountable for their internal control responsibilities.

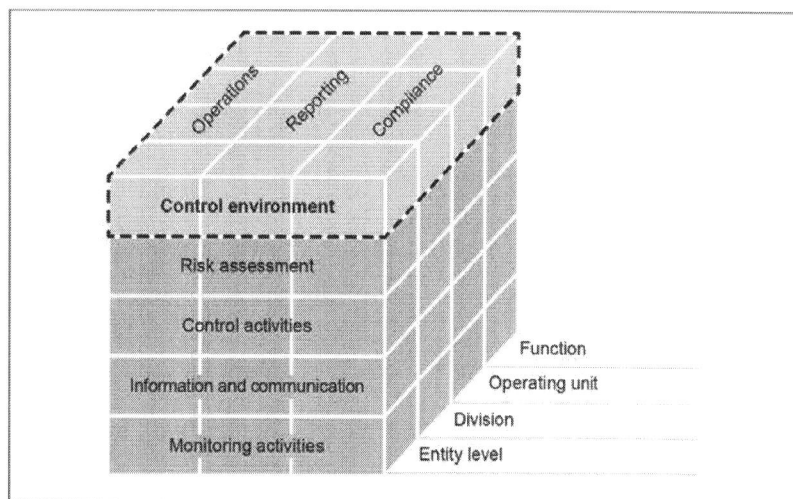

Operations — Reporting — Compliance

Control environment

Risk assessment

Control activities

Information and communication

Monitoring activities

Function
Operating unit
Division
Entity level

Source: COSO.

Principle 1 - Demonstrate Commitment to Integrity and Ethical Values

1.01 The oversight body and management should demonstrate a commitment to integrity and ethical values.

Attributes

1.02 The following attributes contribute to the design, implementation, and operating effectiveness of this principle:

a. Set the Tone at the Top - The oversight body and management should demonstrate the importance of integrity and ethical values through their directives, attitudes, and behavior.

b. Establish Standards of Conduct - Management should define expectations concerning integrity and ethical values in the entity's standards of conduct.

c. Evaluate Adherence to Standards of Conduct - Management should establish processes to evaluate performance against the organization's expected standards of conduct and address any deviations in a timely manner.

Set Tone at the Top

1.03 The oversight body and management should demonstrate the importance of integrity and ethical values through their directives, attitudes, and behavior.

1.04 The oversight body and management lead by an example that demonstrates the organization's values, philosophy, and operating style. The oversight body and management set the tone at the top and throughout the organization by their example, which is fundamental to an effective internal control system. In larger organizations, the various layers of management in the organizational structure can also set "tone in the middle."

1.05 The oversight body and management's directives, attitudes, and behaviors reflect the integrity and ethical values expected throughout the organization. The oversight body and management reinforce the commitment to doing what is right, not just maintaining a minimum level of performance necessary to comply with applicable laws and regulations, so that these priorities are understood by all stakeholders, such as regulators, employees, and the general public.

1.06 Tone at the top can be either a driver, as shown in the preceding paragraphs, or a barrier to internal control. Without a strong tone at the top to support an internal control system, the organization's risk identification may be incomplete, risk responses may be inappropriate, control activities may not be appropriately designed or implemented, information and communication may falter, and results of monitoring may not be understood or acted upon to remediate deficiencies.

Establish Standards of Conduct

1.07 Management should define expectations concerning integrity and ethical values in the entity's standards of conduct.

1.08 Management establishes standards of conduct to communicate expectations concerning integrity and ethical values. The organization uses ethical values to balance the needs and concerns of different stakeholders, such as regulators, employees, and the general public. The standards of conduct guide the directives, attitudes, and behaviors of the organization in achieving the entity's objectives.

1.09 Management, with oversight from the oversight body, defines the organization's expectations of ethical values in the standards of conduct. Management may consider using policies, operating principles, or guidelines to communicate the standards of conduct to the organization.

Evaluate Adherence to Standards of Conduct

1.10 Management should establish processes to evaluate performance against the organization's expected standards of conduct and address any deviations in a timely manner.

1.11 Management uses established standards of conduct as the basis for evaluating adherence to integrity and ethical values across the organization. Management evaluates the adherence to standards of conduct across all levels of the organization. To gain assurance that the entity's standards of conduct are implemented effectively, management evaluates the directives, attitudes, and behaviors of individuals and teams. Evaluations may consist of ongoing monitoring or separate evaluations.[6] Individual personnel can also report issues through reporting lines, such as regular staff meetings, upward feedback processes, a whistle-blowing program, or an ethics hotline.[7] The oversight body evaluates management's adherence to the standards of conduct as well as the overall adherence by the organization.

1.12 Management determines the tolerance level for deviations. Management may determine that the entity will have zero tolerance for deviations from certain expected standards of conduct, while deviations from others may be addressed with warnings to personnel. Management establishes a process for evaluations of individual and team adherence to standards of conduct that escalates and remediates deviations. Management addresses deviations from expected standards of conduct in a timely and consistent manner. Depending on the severity of the deviation determined through the evaluation process, management, with oversight from the oversight body, takes appropriate actions and may also need to consider applicable laws and regulations. The standards of conduct to which management holds personnel, however, remain consistent.

Principle 2 - Exercise Oversight Responsibility

2.01 The oversight body should oversee the entity's internal control system.

Attributes

2.02 The following attributes contribute to the design, implementation, and operating effectiveness of this principle:

a. Establish Oversight Structure - The entity should determine an appropriate oversight structure based on applicable laws and regulations, relevant government guidance, and feedback from key stakeholders.

---

[6] See paras. 16.06 through 16.11 for further discussion of ongoing monitoring and separate evaluations.

[7] See paras. 16.12 through 16.14 for further discussion of internal control issues.

b. Provide Oversight for the Internal Control System - The oversight body should oversee management's design, implementation, and operation of the internal control system.

c. Provide Input for Remediation of Deficiencies - The oversight body should provide input to management's plans for remediation of deficiencies in the internal control system as appropriate.

Establish Oversight Structure

2.03 The entity should determine an appropriate oversight structure based on applicable laws and regulations, relevant government guidance, and feedback from key stakeholders.

2.04 The entity determines an oversight structure to fulfill responsibilities set forth by applicable laws and regulations, relevant government guidance, and feedback from key stakeholders. The entity will select, or if mandated by law will have selected for it, an oversight body. When the oversight body is composed of entity management, activities referenced in the Green Book as performed by "management" exclude such management when in their role as the oversight body.

Responsibilities of an Oversight Body

2.05 When the oversight structure of an entity is led by senior management, senior management may distinguish itself from divisional or functional management through the establishment of an oversight body. An oversight body oversees the entity's operations, provides constructive criticism to management, and where appropriate, makes oversight decisions to ensure that the entity achieves its objectives in alignment with the entity's integrity and ethical values.

Qualifications for an Oversight Body

2.06 In selecting members for an oversight body, the entity or applicable body defines the entity knowledge, relevant expertise, number of members, and possible independence needed to fulfill the oversight responsibilities for the entity.

2.07 Members of an oversight body understand the entity's objectives, related risks, and expectations of its stakeholders. In addition to an oversight body, an organization within the federal government may have several bodies that are key stakeholders for the entity, such as the White House, Congress, OMB, and the Department of the Treasury. An oversight body works with key stakeholders to understand their expectations and help the entity fulfill these expectations if appropriate.

2.08 The entity or applicable body also considers the expertise needed by members to oversee, question, and evaluate management. Capabilities expected of all members of an oversight body include integrity and ethical values, leadership, critical thinking, and problem-solving.

2.09 Further, in determining the number of members of an oversight body, the entity or applicable body considers the need for more specialized skills to enable discussion, offer constructive criticism to management, and make appropriate oversight decisions. Some specialized skills may include:

- Internal control mindset (e.g., professional skepticism, perspectives on approaches for identifying and responding to risks, and assessing the effectiveness of the system of internal control)

- Programmatic expertise, including knowledge of the entity's mission, programs, and operational processes

- Financial expertise, including financial reporting (e.g., accounting standards, financial reporting requirements)

- Relevant systems and technology (e.g., understanding critical systems and technology risks and opportunities)

2.10 If authorized by applicable laws and regulations, the entity may also consider including independent members as part of an oversight body.[8] Members of an oversight body scrutinize and question management's activities, present alternative views, and act when faced with obvious or suspected wrongdoing. Independent members with relevant expertise provide value through their impartial evaluation of the entity and its operations in achieving objectives.

---

[8] See GAO, *Government Auditing Standards: 2011 Revision*, GAO-12-331G (Washington, D.C.: December 2011), paras. 3.02 through 3.59 for further discussion of independence.

Provide Oversight for the System of Internal Control

2.11 The oversight body should oversee management's design, implementation, and operation of the internal control system.

2.12 The oversight body oversees management's design, implementation, and operation of the entity's internal control system. The oversight body's responsibilities for the entity's internal control system include:

- Control Environment - Establish integrity and ethical values, establish oversight structure, develop expectations of competence, and maintain accountability to all members of the oversight body and key stakeholders.

- Risk Assessment - Oversee management's assessment of risks to the achievement of objectives, including the potential impact of significant changes, fraud, and management override of internal control.

- Control Activities - Provide oversight to management in the development and performance of control activities.

- Information and Communication - Analyze and discuss information relating to the entity's achievement of objectives.

- Monitoring - Scrutinize the nature and scope of management's monitoring activities as well as management's evaluation and remediation of identified deficiencies.

2.13 These responsibilities are supported by the organizational structure that management establishes.[9] The oversight body oversees management's design, implementation, and operation of the entity's organizational structure to ensure that the necessary processes to enable the oversight body to fulfill its responsibilities exist and are operating effectively.

Provide Input for Remediation of Deficiencies

2.14 The oversight body should provide input to management's plans for remediation of deficiencies in the internal control system as appropriate.

---

[9] See paras. 3.03 through 3.07 for further discussion of organizational structure.

GAO 13-830SP Green Book Exposure Draft

2.15 Management reports deficiencies identified in the internal control system to the oversight body. The oversight body oversees and provides direction to management on the remediation of these deficiencies. The oversight body also provides direction when a deficiency crosses organizational boundaries or units, or when the interests of management may conflict with remediation efforts. When appropriate and authorized, the oversight body may direct the creation of teams to address or oversee specific matters critical to achieving the entity's objectives.

2.16 The oversight body is responsible for overseeing the remediation of deficiencies as appropriate and for providing direction to management on appropriate time frames for correcting these deficiencies.[10]

Principle 3 - Establish Structure, Responsibility, and Authority

3.01 Management should establish an organizational structure, assign responsibility, and delegate authority to achieve the entity's objectives.

Attributes

3.02 The following attributes contribute to the design, implementation, and operating effectiveness of this principle:

a. Establish Organizational Structure - Management should establish an organizational structure.

b. Assign Responsibility and Delegate Authority - Management should assign responsibility and delegate authority to key roles throughout the organization.

c. Document Internal Control System - Management should develop and maintain documentation of its internal control system.

Establish Organizational Structure

3.03 Management should establish an organizational structure.

---

[10] See paras. 17.09 through 17.10 for further discussion of timely remediation of findings.

3.04 Management establishes an organizational structure necessary to enable the entity to plan, execute, control, and assess the organization in achieving its objectives. Management develops the overall responsibilities from the entity's objectives that enable the entity to achieve its objectives and address related risks.

3.05 Management develops an organizational structure with an understanding of the overall responsibilities, and assigns these responsibilities to discrete units to enable the organization to operate in an efficient and effective manner, comply with applicable laws and regulations, and reliably report quality information.[11] Based on the nature of the assigned responsibility, management chooses the type and number of discrete units, such as divisions, offices, or their related subunits.

3.06 As part of establishing an organizational structure, management considers how units interact in order to fulfill their overall responsibilities. Management establishes reporting lines within an organizational structure so that units can communicate the necessary quality information for each unit to fulfill its overall responsibilities.[12] Reporting lines are defined at all levels of the organization and provide methods of communication that can flow down, across, up, and around the structure.[13] Management also considers the entity's overall responsibilities to external sources and establishes reporting lines that allow the entity to both communicate and receive information from external sources.[14]

3.07 Management periodically evaluates the organizational structure to ensure that it meets the entity's objectives and has adapted to any new objectives for the entity, such as a new regulation.

Assign Responsibility and Delegate Authority

3.08 Management should assign responsibility and delegate authority to key roles throughout the organization.

---

[11] See paras. 13.08 through 13.10 for further discussion of quality information.

[12] See paras. 13.03 through 13.10 for further discussion of quality information.

[13] See paras. 14.03 through 14.08 for further discussion of internal reporting lines.

[14] See paras. 15.03 through 15.08 for further discussion of external reporting lines.

3.09 To achieve the entity's objectives, management assigns responsibility and delegates authority to key roles throughout the organization. A key role is a position in the organizational structure that is assigned an overall responsibility of the entity. Generally, key roles relate to senior management positions within an organization.

3.10 Management considers the overall responsibilities assigned to each unit, determines what key roles are needed to fulfill the assigned responsibilities, and establishes the key roles. Those in key roles can further assign responsibility for internal control to roles below them in the organizational structure, but retain ownership for fulfilling the overall responsibilities assigned to the unit.

3.11 Management determines what level of authority the key role needs to fulfill that responsibility. Management delegates authority only to the extent required to achieve the entity's objectives. As part of delegating authority, management evaluates the delegation to ensure proper segregation of duties within the unit and in the organizational structure. Segregation of duties helps prevent fraud, waste, and abuse in the entity by considering the need to separate authority, custody, and accounting in the organizational structure.[15] As with assigning responsibility, those in key roles can delegate their authority for internal control to roles below them in the organizational structure.

Document Internal Control System

3.12 Management should develop and maintain documentation of its internal control system.

3.13 Management develops and maintains documentation of its internal control system for a number of reasons. Effective documentation assists in management's design of internal control by establishing and communicating the who, what, when, where, and why of internal control execution to personnel. Documentation also provides a means to retain organizational knowledge and mitigate the risk of having that knowledge limited to a few personnel, as well as a means to communicate that knowledge as needed to external parties such as external auditors.

---

[15] See paras. 10.15 through 10.18 for further discussion of segregation of duties.

3.14 Management documents internal control to meet operational needs. Documentation of controls, including changes to controls, is evidence that controls are identified, capable of being communicated to those responsible for their performance, and capable of being monitored and evaluated by the entity. The extent of documentation supporting the design, implementation, and operating effectiveness of the five components of internal control is a matter of judgment for management. Management considers the cost-benefit of documentation requirements for the entity as well as the size, nature, and complexity of the entity and its objectives. Some level of documentation, however, is necessary to ensure that the components of internal control are designed, implemented, and operating effectively.

Principle 4 - Demonstrate Commitment to Competence

4.01 Management should demonstrate a commitment to attract, develop, and retain competent individuals.

Attributes
4.02 The following attributes contribute to the design, implementation, and operating effectiveness of this principle:

a. Establish Expectations of Competence - Management should establish expectations of competence throughout the organization.

b. Attract, Develop, and Retain Individuals - Management should attract, develop, and retain competent personnel.

c. Plan and Prepare for Succession - Management should define succession and contingency plans for key roles in the organization.

Establish Expectations of Competence

4.03 Management should establish expectations of competence throughout the organization.

4.04 Management establishes expectations of competence for key roles, and other roles at management's discretion, to help the entity achieve its objectives. Competence is the qualification to carry out assigned responsibilities. It requires relevant knowledge, skills, and abilities, which are gained largely from professional experience, training, and certifications. It is expressed in the attitude and behavior of individuals as they carry out their responsibilities.

4.05 Management considers standards of conduct, assigned responsibility, and delegated authority when establishing expectations. Management establishes expectations of competence for key roles. Management may also establish expectations of competence for all personnel through policies within the organization's internal control system.[16]

4.06 Personnel need to possess and maintain a level of competence that allows them to accomplish their assigned responsibilities, as well as understand the importance of effective internal control. Holding individuals accountable to established policies by evaluating personnel's competence is integral to attracting, developing, and retaining individuals. Management evaluates competence of personnel across the organization in relation to established policies. Management acts as necessary to address any deviations from the established policies. The oversight body evaluates the competence of management as well as the overall competence of the organization.

Attract, Develop, and Retain Individuals

4.07 Management should attract, develop, and retain competent personnel.

4.08 Management attracts, develops, and retains competent personnel to achieve the entity's objectives. Management may consider:

- Attract - Conduct procedures to determine whether a particular candidate fits the organizational needs and has the competence for the proposed role.

- Train - Enable individuals to develop competencies appropriate for key roles, reinforce standards of conduct, and tailor training based on the needs of the role.

- Mentor - Provide guidance on the individual's performance based on standards of conduct and expectations of competence, align the individual's skills and expertise with the entity's objectives, and help personnel adapt to an evolving environment.

---

[16] See paras. 12.03 through 12.05 for further discussion of policies.

- Retain – Provide incentives to motivate and reinforce expected levels of performance and desired conduct, including training and credentialing as appropriate.

Plan and Prepare for Succession

4.09 Management should define succession and contingency plans for key roles in the organization.

4.10 Management defines succession and contingency plans for key roles to help the organization continue achieving its objectives. Succession plans address the entity's need to replace competent personnel over the long term, whereas contingency plans address the organization's need to respond to sudden personnel changes impacting the organization that could compromise the internal control system.

4.11 Management defines succession plans for key roles, chooses succession candidates, and trains succession candidates to assume the key roles. If management relies on a service organization to fulfill the assigned responsibilities of key roles in the entity, management assesses whether the service organization can continue in these key roles, identifies other candidate organizations for the roles, and ensures that processes are in place to enable knowledge sharing with the succession candidate organization.

4.12 Management defines contingency plans for assigning responsibilities if a key role in the organization is vacated without advance notice. The importance of the key role in the internal control system and the impact to the organization of its vacancy dictates the formality and depth of the contingency plan.

Principle 5 - Enforce Accountability

5.01 Management should evaluate performance and hold individuals accountable for their internal control responsibilities.

Attributes

5.02 The following attributes contribute to the design, implementation, and operating effectiveness of this principle:

a. Enforce Accountability - Management should enforce accountability for performance of internal control responsibilities.

b. Consider Excessive Pressures - Management should evaluate and adjust pressures on personnel related to achieving objectives as they assign responsibilities and evaluate performance.

Enforce Accountability

5.03 Management should enforce accountability for performance of internal control responsibilities.

5.04 Management enforces accountability of individuals performing their internal control responsibilities. Accountability is driven by the tone at the top and supported by the commitment to integrity and ethical values, organizational structure, and expectations of competence, which influence the control culture of the organization. Accountability for performance of internal control responsibility supports day-to-day decision making, attitudes, and behaviors. Management holds personnel accountable through mechanisms such as performance appraisals and disciplinary actions.

5.05 Management holds entity personnel accountable for performing their assigned internal control responsibilities. The oversight body, in turn, holds management accountable as well as the organization as a whole for its internal control responsibilities.

5.06 If management establishes incentives, management recognizes that actions can yield unintended consequences and evaluates incentives to ensure that they align with the entity's standards of conduct.

5.07 Management holds service organizations accountable for their assigned internal control responsibilities. Management may contract service organizations to perform roles in the organizational structure. Management communicates to the service organization the objectives of the entity and their related risks, the entity's standards of conduct, the role of the service organization in the organizational structure, the assigned responsibilities and authorities of the role, and the expectations of competence for its role that will enable the service organization to perform its internal control responsibilities.

5.08 Management, with oversight from the oversight body, takes corrective action as necessary to enforce accountability for internal control in the organization. These actions can range from informal feedback provided by the direct supervisor to disciplinary action taken by the oversight body depending on the significance of the deficiency to the internal control system.[17]

Consider Excessive Pressures

5.09 Management should evaluate and adjust pressures on personnel related to achieving objectives as they assign responsibilities and evaluate performance.

5.10 Management adjusts excessive pressures on personnel in the organization. Pressure can appear in an organization due to goals established by management to meet objectives or cyclical demands of various processes performed by the organization, such as year-end financial statement preparation. Excessive pressure can result in personnel "cutting corners" to meet the established goals.

5.11 Management is responsible for evaluating pressure on personnel to help personnel fulfill their assigned responsibilities in accordance with the entity's standards of conduct. Management can adjust excessive pressures using many different tools, such as rebalancing workloads or increasing resource levels.

---

[17] See Overview: Effect on the Internal Control System for further discussion of significance of deficiencies.

Risk Assessment

Overview

Having established an effective control environment, management assesses the risks facing the entity as it seeks to achieve its objectives. This assessment provides the basis for developing appropriate risk responses. Management assesses the risks the entity faces from both external and internal sources.

Principles

6. Management should define objectives and risk tolerances.

7. Management should identify, analyze, and respond to risks related to achieving the defined objectives.

8. Management should consider the potential for fraud when identifying, analyzing, and responding to risks.

9. Management should identify, analyze, and respond to significant changes in the internal control system.

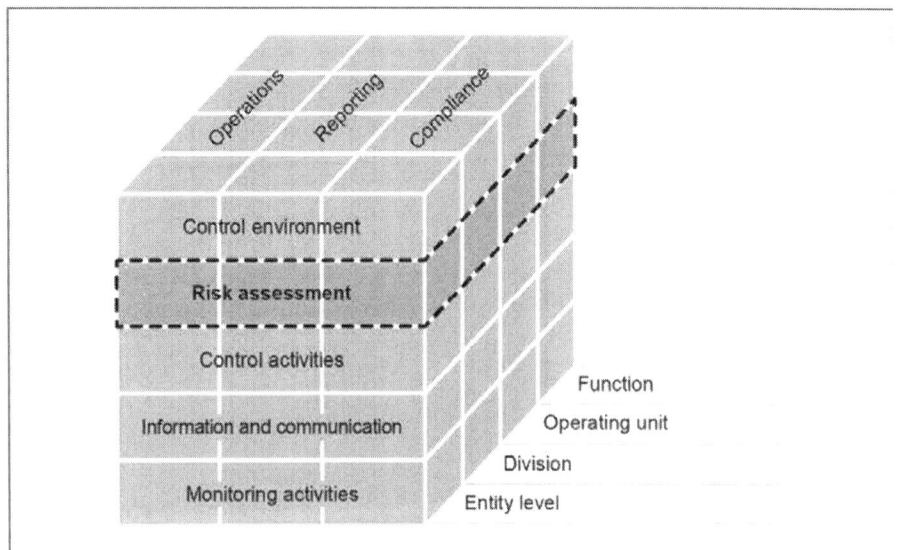

Source: COSO.

Principle 6 - Define Objectives and Risk Tolerances

6.01 Management should define objectives and risk tolerances.

Attributes

6.02 The following attributes contribute to the design, implementation, and operating effectiveness of this principle:

a. Define Objectives - Management should define objectives in specific and measurable terms to enable the design of internal control for related risks.

b. Define Risk Tolerances - Management should define the risk tolerances for the defined objectives.

Define Objectives

6.03 Management should define objectives in specific and measurable terms to enable the design of internal control for related risks.

6.04 Management defines objectives in specific and measurable terms to enable the design of internal control for related risks. Specific terms are fully and clearly set forth so they can be easily understood. Measurable terms allow for the assessment of performance toward achieving objectives. Objectives are initially set as part of the objective-setting process and then refined as they are incorporated into the internal control system when management uses them to establish the control environment.

6.05 Management defines objectives in specific terms so they are understood at all levels of the entity. This involves clearly defining what is to be achieved, who is to achieve it, how it will be achieved, and the time frames for achievement. All objectives can be broadly classified into one or more of three categories: operations, reporting, or compliance. Reporting objectives are further categorized as being either internal or external, and financial or nonfinancial. Management ensures that the defined objectives align with the organization's mission, strategic plan and performance goals.

GAO 13-830SP Green Book Exposure Draft

6.06 Management defines objectives in measurable terms so that performance toward achieving those objectives can be assessed. Measurable objectives are generally free of bias and do not require subjective judgments to dominate their measurement. Measurable objectives are also stated in a quantitative or qualitative form that permits reasonably consistent measurement.

6.07 Management considers external requirements and internal expectations when defining objectives to enable the design of internal control. Legislators, regulators, and standard-setting bodies set external requirements by establishing the laws, regulations, and standards with which the organization is required to comply. Management identifies, understands, and incorporates these requirements into the entity's objectives. Management sets internal expectations and requirements through the established standards of conduct,[18] oversight structure,[19] organizational structure,[20] and expectations of competence[21] as part of the control environment.

6.08 Management evaluates and, if necessary, revises defined objectives to ensure that they are consistent with these requirements and expectations. This consistency enables management to identify and analyze risks associated with achieving the defined objectives.

6.09 Management determines whether performance measures for the defined objectives are appropriate for evaluating the entity's performance in achieving those objectives. For quantitative objectives, performance measures may be a targeted percentage or numerical value. For qualitative objectives, management may need to design performance measures that indicate a level or degree of performance, such as milestones.

Define Risk Tolerances

6.10 Management should define the risk tolerances for the defined objectives.

---

[18] See paras. 1.07 through 1.09 for further discussion of standards of conduct.

[19] See paras. 2.03 through 2.10 for further discussion of oversight structure.

[20] See paras. 3.03 through 3.07 for further discussion of organizational structure.

[21] See paras. 4.03 through 4.06 for further discussion of expectations of competence.

6.11 Management defines risk tolerances for the defined objectives. Risk tolerance is the acceptable level of variation in performance relative to the achievement of objectives. Risk tolerances are initially set as part of the objective-setting process. Management defines the risk tolerances for defined objectives by ensuring that the set levels of variation for performance measures are appropriate for the design of an internal control system.

6.12 Management defines risk tolerances in specific and measurable terms so they are clearly stated and can be measured. Risk tolerance is often measured in the same unit as the performance measures for the defined objectives. Depending on the category of objectives, risk tolerances may be expressed as follows:

- Operations and Compliance Objectives - Acceptable level of variation in performance in relation to risk.

- Nonfinancial Reporting Objectives - Required level of precision and accuracy suitable for user needs.

- Financial Reporting Objectives - Material misstatements, including omissions, are those that, either individually or in the aggregate, could reasonably be expected to influence the decisions of financial statement users. Judgments about materiality are made in light of surrounding circumstances, involve both qualitative and quantitative considerations, and are affected by the needs of financial statement users and size or nature of a misstatement.

6.13 Management also evaluates whether risk tolerances enable the appropriate design of internal control by considering whether they are consistent with requirements and expectations for the defined objectives. As in defining objectives, management considers the risk tolerances in the context of the entity's applicable laws, regulations, and standards as well as the entity's standards of conduct, oversight structure, organizational structure, and expectations of competence. If risk tolerances for defined objectives are not consistent with these requirements and expectations, management revises the risk tolerances to achieve consistency.

Principle 7 – Identify, Analyze, and Respond to Risk

7.01 Management should identify, analyze, and respond to risks related to achieving the defined objectives.

Attributes

7.02 The following attributes contribute to the design, implementation, and operating effectiveness of this principle:

a. Identify Risks - Management should identify risks throughout the entity.

b. Analyze Risks - Management should analyze the identified risks to estimate their significance.

c. Respond to Risks - Management should design responses to the analyzed risks.

Identify Risks

7.03 Management should identify risks throughout the entity.

7.04 Management identifies risks throughout the entity to provide a basis for analyzing risks. Risk assessment is the identification and analysis of risks related to achieving the defined objectives to form a basis for designing risk responses.

7.05 To identify risks, management considers the types of risks that impact the entity. This includes both inherent and residual risk. Inherent risk is the risk to an entity in the absence of management's response to the risk. Residual risk is the risk that remains after management's response to inherent risk. Both risks could cause deficiencies in the internal control system.

7.06 Management considers all significant interactions within the entity and with external parties, changes within the entity's internal and external environment,[22] and other internal and external factors to identify risks throughout the entity. Internal risk factors may include the complex nature of an entity's programs, its organizational structure, or the use of new technology in operational processes. External risk factors may include new or amended laws, regulations, or professional standards; economic instability; or potential natural disasters. Management considers these factors at both the entity and transaction level to comprehensively identify risks that affect defined objectives.[23] Risk identification methods may

---

[22] See paras. 9.03 through 9.05 for further discussion of changes in the internal control system.

[23] See paras. 10.10 through 10.14 for further discussion of level of controls.

include qualitative and quantitative ranking activities, management conferences, forecasting and strategic planning, and consideration of deficiencies identified through audits and other assessments.

Analyze Risks

7.07 Management should analyze the identified risks to estimate their significance.

7.08 Management analyzes the identified risks to estimate their significance, which provides a basis for responding to the risks. Significance refers to the effect on achieving a defined objective.

7.09 Management estimates the significance of the identified risks to assess their effect on achieving the defined objectives at both the entity and transaction level. Management estimates the significance of a risk by considering the magnitude of impact, likelihood of occurrence, and nature of the risk. Magnitude of impact refers to the likely magnitude of deficiency that could result from the risk and is affected by factors such as the size, pace, and duration of the risk's impact. Likelihood of occurrence refers to the possibility that a risk will occur. The nature of the risk involves factors such as the degree of subjectivity involved with the risk and whether the risk arises from fraud or from complex or unusual transactions. The oversight body may oversee management's estimates of significance to ensure that risk tolerances have been properly defined.

7.10 Risks may either be analyzed on an individual basis or grouped into categories with related risks and analyzed collectively. Regardless of whether risks are analyzed individually or collectively, management considers the correlation among different risks or groups of risks when estimating their significance. The specific risk analysis methodology used can vary by entity because of differences in entities' missions and the difficulty in qualitatively and quantitatively defining risk tolerances.

Respond to Risks

7.11 Management should design responses to the analyzed risks.

7.12 Management designs responses to the analyzed risks so that risks are within the defined risk tolerance for the defined objective. Management designs overall risk responses for the analyzed risks based on the significance of the risk and defined risk tolerance. These risk responses may include:

- Acceptance - No action is taken to respond to the risk.

- Avoidance - Action is taken to stop the operational process or the part of the operational process causing the risk.

- Reduction - Action is taken to reduce the likelihood or magnitude of the risk.

- Sharing - Action is taken to transfer or share risks across the entity or with external parties, such as insuring against losses.

7.13 Based on the selected risk response, management designs the specific actions to respond to the analyzed risks. The nature and extent of risk response actions depend on the defined risk tolerance. Operating within the defined risk tolerance provides greater assurance that the entity will achieve its objectives. Performance measures are used to assess whether risk response actions enable the entity to operate within the defined risk tolerances. When risk response actions do not enable the entity to operate within the defined risk tolerances, management may need to revise risk responses or reconsider defined risk tolerances.

Principle 8 - Assess Fraud Risk

8.01 Management should consider the potential for fraud when identifying, analyzing, and responding to risks.[24]

Attributes

8.02 The following attributes contribute to the design, implementation, and operating effectiveness of this principle:

a. Consider Types of Fraud - Management should consider the types of fraud that can occur within the organization.

---

[24] Fraud involves obtaining something of value through willful misrepresentation. Whether an act is in fact fraud is a determination to be made through the judicial or other adjudicative system and is beyond management's professional responsibility for assessing risk.

b. Consider Fraud Risk Factors - Management should consider fraud risk factors.

c. Respond to Fraud Risks - Management should analyze and respond to identified fraud risks.

Consider Types of Fraud

8.03 Management should consider the types of fraud that can occur within the organization.

8.04 Management considers the types of fraud that can occur within the organization to provide a basis for identifying fraud risks. Fraud can occur in:

- Fraudulent Financial Reporting - Intentional misstatements or omissions of amounts or disclosures in financial statements to deceive financial statement users. This could include intentional alteration of accounting records, misrepresentation of transactions, intentional misapplication of accounting principles, or other means.

- Misappropriation of Assets - Theft of an entity's assets. This could include theft of property, embezzlement of receipts, fraudulent payments, or other means.

- Corruption - Bribery and other illegal acts.

8.05 In addition to fraud, management considers other forms of misconduct that can occur, such as waste and abuse. Waste is the act of using or expending resources carelessly, extravagantly, or to no purpose. Abuse involves behavior that is deficient or improper when compared with behavior that a prudent person would consider reasonable and necessary operational practice given the facts and circumstances. This includes the misuse of authority or position for personal gain or for the benefit of another. Waste and abuse do not necessarily involve fraud or illegal acts. However, they may be an indication of potential fraud or illegal acts and may still impact the achievement of defined objectives.

Consider Fraud Risk Factors

8.06 Management should consider fraud risk factors.

8.07 Management considers fraud risk factors. Fraud risk factors do not necessarily indicate that fraud exists but are often present when fraud occurs. Fraud risk factors include:

- Incentive/pressure - Management or other personnel have an incentive or are under pressure, which provides a motive to commit fraud.[25]

- Opportunity - Circumstances exist, such as the absence of controls, ineffective controls, or the ability of management to override controls, that provide an opportunity to commit fraud.

- Attitude/rationalization - Individuals involved are able to rationalize committing fraud. Some individuals possess an attitude, character, or ethical values that allow them to knowingly and intentionally commit a dishonest act.

8.08 Management uses the fraud risk factors to identify fraud risks. While fraud risk may be greatest when all three risk factors are present, one or more of these factors may indicate a fraud risk. Other information provided by internal and external parties can also be used to identify fraud risks. This may include allegations of fraud or suspected fraud reported by the OIG or internal auditors, personnel, or external parties that interact with the organization.

Respond to Fraud Risks

8.09 Management should analyze and respond to identified fraud risks.

8.10 Management analyzes and responds to identified fraud risks to ensure that they are effectively mitigated. Fraud risks are analyzed through the same risk analysis process performed for all identified risks.[26] Management analyzes the identified fraud risks by estimating their significance, both individually and in the aggregate, to assess their effect on achieving the defined objectives. As part of analyzing fraud risk, management also assesses the risk of management override of controls.[27] The oversight body oversees management's assessments of fraud risk and the risk of management override of controls to ensure that they are appropriate.

---

[25] See paras. 5.09 through 5.11 for further discussion of pressure.

[26] See paras. 7.07 through 7.10 for further discussion of analyzing risks.

[27] See para. 10.17 for further discussion of management override.

8.11 Management responds to fraud risks through the same risk response process performed for all analyzed risks.[28] Management designs an overall risk response and specific actions for responding to fraud risks. It may be possible to reduce or eliminate certain fraud risks by making changes to the entity's activities and processes. These changes may include stopping or reorganizing certain operations and reallocating roles among personnel to enhance segregation of duties. In addition to responding to fraud risks, management may need to develop further responses to address the risk of management override of controls. Further, when fraud has been detected, it may be necessary to revise the risk assessment process going forward.

Principle 9 – Identify, Analyze, and Respond to Change

9.01 Management should identify, analyze, and respond to significant changes in the internal control system.

Attributes

9.02 The following attributes contribute to the design, implementation, and operating effectiveness of this principle:

a. Identify Change - Management should identify changes that could significantly impact the entity's internal control system.

b. Analyze and Respond to Change - Management should analyze and respond to identified changes that impact the entity's internal control system.

Identify Change

9.03 Management should identify changes that could significantly impact the entity's internal control system.

9.04 As part of risk assessment or a similar process, management identifies changes that could significantly impact the entity's internal control system. Identifying, analyzing, and responding to change is

---

[28] See paras. 7.11 through 7.13 for further discussion of responding to risks.

similar to, if not part of, the entity's regular risk assessment process. However, change is discussed separately because it is critical to an effective internal control system and can often be overlooked or inadequately addressed in the normal course of operations.

9.05 Conditions affecting the entity and its environment continually change. Management can anticipate and plan for significant changes by using a forward-looking process for identifying change. Management identifies, on a timely basis, significant changes to internal and external conditions that have already occurred or are expected to occur. Changes in internal conditions include changes to the entity's programs or activities, oversight structure, organizational structure, personnel, and technology. Changes in external conditions include changes in the governmental, economic, technological, legal, regulatory, and physical environments. Identified significant changes are communicated across the organization through established reporting lines to appropriate personnel.[29]

Analyze and Respond to Change

9.06 Management should analyze and respond to identified changes that impact the entity's internal control system.

9.07 As part of risk assessment or a similar process, management analyzes and responds to identified changes and related risks to ensure the effectiveness of the internal control system. Changes in conditions affecting the entity and its environment often require changes to the entity's internal control system, as existing controls may not be effective for meeting objectives or addressing risks under changed conditions. Management analyzes the effect of identified changes on the internal control system and responds by revising the internal control system on a timely basis, when necessary, to ensure its effectiveness.

9.08 Further, changing conditions often prompt new risks or changes to existing risks that need to be assessed. As part of analyzing and responding to change, management performs a risk assessment to identify, analyze, and respond to any new risks prompted by the changes. Additionally, existing risks may require further assessment to determine whether the defined risk tolerances and risk responses need to be revised.

---

[29] See paras. 14.03 through 14.08 for further discussion of internal reporting lines.

Control Activities

Overview

Control activities are the actions management establishes through policies and procedures to achieve objectives and respond to risks in the internal control system, which includes the entity's information system.

Principles

10. Management should design control activities to achieve objectives and risk responses.

11. Management should design control activities for the entity's information system.

12. Management should implement control activities.

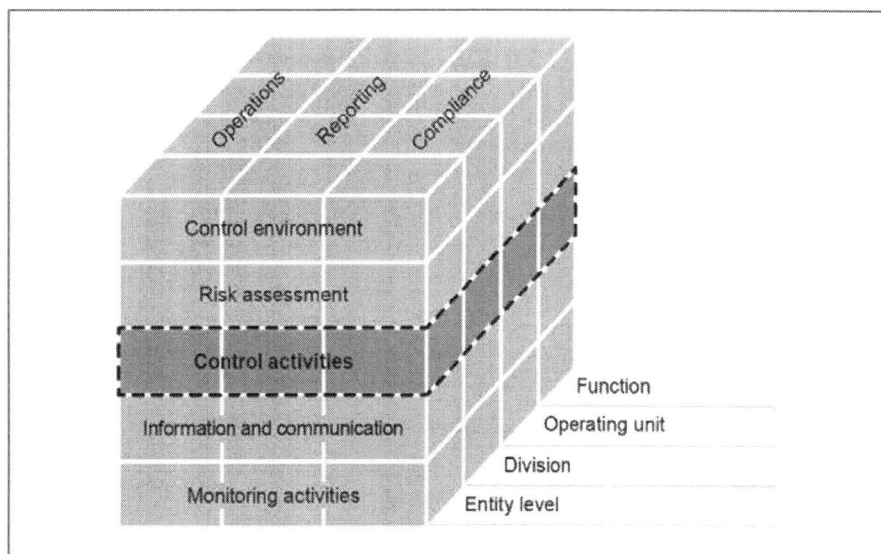

Source: COSO.

Principle 10 - Design Control Activities

10.01 Management should design control activities to achieve objectives and risk responses.

Attributes

10.02 The following attributes contribute to the design, implementation, and operating effectiveness of this principle:

a. Respond to Objectives and Risks - Management should design control activities that respond to the entity's objectives and risks.

b. Design the Types of Control Activities - Management should design appropriate types of control activities needed for the entity's internal control system.

c. Design Control Activities at Various Levels - Management should design control activities at appropriate levels in the organizational structure.

d. Consider Segregation of Duties - Management should consider segregation of duties in designing the assignment of control activity responsibilities.

Respond to Objectives and Risks

10.03 Management should design control activities that respond to the entity's objectives and risks.

10.04 Management designs control activities in response to the entity's objectives and risks to achieve an effective internal control system. Control activities are the policies, procedures, techniques, and mechanisms that enforce management's directives to achieve the entity's objectives and address related risks. As part of the control environment component, management defines responsibilities, assigns them to key roles, and delegates authority to achieve the entity's objectives. As part of the risk assessment component, management identifies the risks related to the entity and its objectives including its service organizations, the entity's risk tolerance, and risk responses. Management designs control activities to fulfill defined responsibilities and address identified risk responses.

Design Appropriate Types of Control Activities

10.05 Management should design appropriate types of control activities needed for the entity's internal control system.

10.06 Management designs appropriate types of control activities for the entity's internal control system. Control activities help management fulfill responsibilities and address identified risk responses in the internal control system.

> **Common Categories of Internal Control**
>
> Examples of common categories of control activities include the following:
>
> - Top Level Reviews of Actual Performance
> - Reviews by Management at the Functional or Activity Level
> - Management of Human Capital
> - Controls over Information Processing
> - Physical control over vulnerable assets
> - Establishment and Review of Performance Measures and Indicators
> - Segregation of Duties
> - Proper Execution of Transactions and Events
> - Accurate and Timely Recording of Transactions and Events
> - Access Restrictions to and Accountability for Resources and Records
> - Appropriate Documentation of Transactions and Internal Control

Top Level Reviews of Actual Performance

Management tracks major entity achievements and compares these to the plans, goals, and objectives set by the entity.

Reviews by Management at the Functional or Activity Level

Management compares actual performance to planned or expected results throughout the organization and analyzes significant differences.

Management of Human Capital

Effective management of an organization's workforce, its human capital, is essential to achieving results and an important part of internal control. Only when the right personnel for the job are on board and are provided the right training, tools, structure, incentives, and responsibilities is operational success possible. Management ensures that the knowledge, skills, and ability needs are continually assessed and that the organization is able to obtain a workforce that has the required knowledge, skills, and abilities necessary to achieve organizational goals. Training should be aimed at developing and retaining employee knowledge, skills, and abilities to meet changing organizational needs. Management provides qualified and continuous supervision to ensure that internal control objectives are achieved. Management designs performance evaluation and feedback, supplemented by an effective reward system, to help employees understand the connection between their performance and the entity's success. As a part of its human capital planning, management also considers how best to retain valuable employees, plan for their eventual succession, and ensure continuity of needed skills and abilities.

Controls over Information Processing

A variety of control activities are used in information processing. Examples include edit checks of data entered, accounting for transactions in numerical sequences, comparing file totals with control accounts, and controlling access to data, files, and programs. Further guidance on control activities for information processing is provided below under "Control Activities Specific for Information Systems" and in Principle 11.

Physical Control over Vulnerable Assets

Management establishes physical control to secure and safeguard vulnerable assets. Examples include security for and limited access to assets such as cash, securities, inventories, and equipment that might be vulnerable to risk of loss or unauthorized use. Management periodically counts and compares such assets to control records.

Establishment and Review of Performance Measures and Indicators

Management establishes activities to monitor performance measures and indicators. These may include comparisons and assessments relating different sets of data to one another so that analyses of the relationships can be made and appropriate actions taken. Management designs controls aimed at validating the propriety and integrity of both entity and individual performance measures and indicators.

Segregation of Duties

Management divides or segregates key duties and responsibilities among different people to reduce the risk of error, misuse, or fraud. This includes separating the responsibilities for authorizing transactions, processing and recording them, reviewing the transactions, and handling any related assets. Management ensures that no one individual controls all key aspects of a transaction or event.

Proper Execution of Transactions and Events

Transactions and other significant events are authorized and executed only by persons acting within the scope of their authority. This is the principal means of assuring that only valid transactions to exchange, transfer, use, or commit resources and other events are initiated or entered into. Management clearly communicates authorizations to personnel.

Accurate and Timely Recording of Transactions and Events

Management ensures that transactions are promptly recorded to maintain their relevance and value to management in controlling operations and making decisions. This applies to the entire process or life cycle of a transaction or event from its initiation and authorization through its final classification in summary records. In addition, management designs control activities to help ensure that all transactions are completely and accurately recorded.

Access Restrictions to and Accountability for Resources and Records

Management limits access to resources and records to authorized individuals, and assigns and maintains accountability for their custody and use. Management may periodically compare resources with the recorded accountability to help reduce the risk of errors, fraud, misuse, or unauthorized alteration.

Appropriate Documentation of Transactions and Internal Control

Management clearly documents internal control and all transactions and other significant events, and ensures that the documentation is readily available for examination. The documentation may appear in management directives, administrative policies, or operating manuals, in either paper or electronic form. Documentation and records are properly managed and maintained.

10.07 Control activities can be either preventive or detective. The main difference between preventive and detective control activities is when the control activity occurs in an entity's operations. A preventive control activity prevents an entity from failing to achieve an objective or addressing a risk. A detective control activity discovers when an entity is not achieving an objective or addressing a risk before the entity's operation has concluded and corrects the actions so that the entity achieves the objective or addresses the risk.

10.08 Management evaluates the purpose of the control activity as well as the effect a deficiency would have on the entity in achieving its objectives. If the control activity is for a significant purpose or the impact of a deficiency would be significant to achieving the entity's objectives, management may design both preventive and detective control activities.

10.09 Control activities can be implemented in either an automated or a manual manner. Automated control activities are either wholly or partially automated through the entity's information technology. Manual control activities are performed by individuals with minor use of the entity's information technology. Automated control activities tend to be more reliable because they are less susceptible to human error and are typically more efficient.[30] If the entity relies on information technology in its operations, management designs control activities to ensure that the information technology continues to operate properly.

Design Control Activities at Various Levels

10.10 Management should design control activities at the appropriate levels in the organizational structure.

10.11 Management designs control activities to ensure the appropriate coverage of objectives and risks in the operations. Operational processes transform inputs into outputs to achieve the organization's objectives. Management designs entity-level control activities, transaction control activities, or both depending on the level of precision needed to ensure that the entity meets its objectives and addresses related risks.

10.12 Entity-level controls are controls that have a pervasive effect on an organization's internal control system and may pertain to multiple components. Entity-level controls may include controls related to the entity's risk assessment process, control environment, service

---

[30] See paras. 11.07 through 11.10 for further discussion of control activities.

organizations, management override, monitoring, and year-end financial reporting.

10.13 Transaction control activities are actions built directly into operational processes to support the organization in achieving its objectives and addressing related risks. The term "transactions" tends to be associated with financial processes (e.g., payables transactions), while the term "activities" is more generally applied to operational or compliance processes. For the purposes of this standard, "transactions" covers both definitions. Management may design a variety of transaction control activities for operational processes, which may include verifications, reconciliations, authorizations and approvals, physical control activities, and supervisory control activities.

10.14 When choosing between entity-level and transaction control activities, management evaluates the level of precision needed for the operational processes to meet the organization's objectives and address related risks. In determining the necessary level of precision for a control activity, management evaluates:

- Purpose of the control activity - A control activity that functions to prevent or detect generally is more precise than a control activity that merely identifies and explains differences.

- Level of aggregation - A control activity that is performed at a more granular level generally is more precise than one performed at a higher level. For example, an analysis of obligations by budget object class normally is more precise than an analysis of total obligations for the organization.

- Consistency of performance - A control activity that is performed routinely and consistently generally is more precise than one performed sporadically.

- Correlation to relevant operational processes - A control activity that is directly related to an operational process generally is more likely to prevent or detect than a control activity that is only indirectly related.

Consider Segregation of Duties

10.15 Management should consider segregation of duties in designing the assignment of control activity responsibilities.

10.16 Management considers segregation of duties in designing control activity responsibilities to ensure that incompatible duties are segregated and, where such segregation is not practical, designs alternative control activities to address the risk.

10.17 Segregation of duties helps prevent fraud, waste, and abuse in the internal control system.[31] Management considers the need to separate control activities related to authority, custody, and accounting of operations to achieve adequate segregation of duties. In particular, segregation of duties can address the risk of management override. Management override circumvents existing control activities and is a means of committing fraud. Management addresses this risk through segregation of duties, but cannot absolutely prevent it due to the risk of collusion, where two employees collude to commit fraud.

10.18 If segregation of duties is not practical within an operational process due to limited personnel or other factors, management designs alternative control activities to address the risk of fraud, waste, or abuse in the operational process.

Principle 11 – Design Activities for the Information System

11.01 Management should design control activities for the entity's information system.

Attributes

11.02 The following attributes contribute to the design, implementation, and operating effectiveness of this principle:

a. Design the Entity's Information System - Management should design the entity's information system to respond to the entity's objectives and risks.

b. Design Appropriate Types of Control Activities - Management should design appropriate types of control activities in the entity's information system.

---

[31] See paras. 8.03 through 8.05 for further discussion of fraud, waste, and abuse.

c. Design the Information Technology Infrastructure - Management should design control activities over the information technology infrastructure.

d. Design Security Management - Management should design control activities for security management over the entity's information system.

e. Design Information Technology Acquisition, Development, and Maintenance - Management should design control activities over the acquisition, development, and maintenance of information technology.

Design the Entity's Information System

11.03 Management should design the entity's information system to respond to the entity's objectives and risks.

11.04 Management designs the entity's information system to obtain and process information to meet each operational process's information requirements and to respond to the entity's objectives and risks. An information system is the people, processes, data, and technology management organizes to obtain, communicate, or dispose of information. An information system represents the life cycle of information used for the entity's operational processes that enables the entity to obtain, store, and process quality information. An information system includes both manual and technology-enabled information processes. Technology-enabled information processes are commonly referred to as information technology. As part of the control environment component, management defines responsibilities, assigns them to key roles, and delegates authority to achieve the entity's objectives. As part of the risk assessment component, management identifies the risks related to the entity and its objectives including its service organizations, the entity's risk tolerance, and risk responses. Management designs control activities to fulfill defined responsibilities and address the identified risk responses for the entity's information system.

11.05 Management designs the entity's information system and the use of information technology by considering the defined information requirements for each of the entity's operational processes.[32] Information technology enables information related to operational processes to become more available to the entity on a timely basis. Additionally, information technology may enhance internal control over

---

[32] See paras. 13.03 through 13.05 for further discussion of defined information requirements.

security and confidentiality of information by appropriately restricting access. Although information technology implies specific types of control activities, information technology is not a "stand-alone" control consideration. It is an integral part of most control activities.

11.06 Management also evaluates information processing objectives to meet the defined information requirements. Information processing objectives may include:

- Completeness - Transactions that occur are recorded and not understated.

- Accuracy - Transactions are recorded at the correct amount in the right account (and on a timely basis) at each stage of processing.

- Validity - Recorded transactions represent economic events that actually occurred and were executed according to prescribed procedures.

Design Appropriate Types of Control Activities

11.07 Management should design appropriate types of control activities in the entity's information system.

11.08 Management designs appropriate types of control activities in the entity's information system to ensure coverage of information processing objectives for operational processes. For information systems, there are two main types of control activities: general and application control activities.

11.09 Information system general controls (entity-wide, system, and application levels) are the policies and procedures that apply to all or a large segment of an entity's information systems. General controls help ensure the proper operation of information systems by creating the environment for proper operation of application controls. General controls include security management, logical and physical access, configuration management, segregation of duties, and contingency planning.

11.10 Application controls, sometimes referred to as business process controls, are those controls that are incorporated directly into computer applications to help ensure the validity, completeness, accuracy, and confidentiality of transactions and data during application processing.

Application controls include controls over input, processing, output, master file, interface, and data management system controls.

Design the Information Technology Infrastructure

11.11 Management should design control activities over the information technology infrastructure.

11.12 Management designs control activities over the information technology infrastructure to support the completeness, accuracy, and validity of information processing by information technology. Information technology requires an infrastructure in which to operate, including communication networks for linking information technologies, computing resources for applications to operate, and electricity to power the information technology. An entity's information technology infrastructure can be complex. It may be shared by different units within the entity or outsourced either to service organizations or to location-independent technology services (e.g., cloud computing). Management evaluates the objectives of the entity and related risks in designing control activities over the information technology infrastructure.

11.13 Management continues to evaluate changes in the use of information technology and designs new control activities when these changes are incorporated into the entity's information technology infrastructure. Management also designs control activities needed to maintain the information technology infrastructure. Maintaining technology often includes backup and recovery procedures, as well as continuity of operations plans, depending on the risks and consequences of a full or partial power systems outage.

Design Security Management

11.14 Management should design control activities for security management over the entity's information system.

11.15 Management designs control activities for security management over the entity's information system to ensure appropriate access by internal and external sources to protect the entity's information system. Objectives for security management include confidentiality, integrity and availability. Confidentiality means that data, reports and other outputs are safeguarded against unauthorized access. Integrity means that information is guarded against improper modification or destruction, which includes ensuring information's nonrepudiation and authenticity. Availability means that data, reports, and other relevant information are readily available to users when needed.

11.16 Security management includes the information processes and control activities related to access rights in an entity's information technology, including who has the ability to execute transactions. Security management includes access rights across various levels of data, operating system (system software), network, application, and physical layers. Management designs control activities over access to protect an entity from inappropriate access and unauthorized use of the system. These control activities support appropriate segregation of duties. By preventing unauthorized use of and changes to the system, data and program integrity are protected from malicious intent (e.g., someone breaking into the technology to commit fraud, vandalism, or terrorism) or error.

11.17 Management evaluates security threats to information technology, which can be from both internal and external sources. External threats are particularly important for entities that depend on telecommunications networks and the Internet. External threats have become prevalent in today's highly interconnected business environments, and continual effort is required to address these risks. Internal threats may come from former or disgruntled employees. They pose unique risks because they may be both motivated to work against the entity and better equipped to succeed in carrying out a malicious act as they have greater access to and knowledge of the entity's security management systems and processes.

11.18 Management designs control activities to limit user access to information technology through authorization control activities where a unique user identification or token is authorized by an approved list. These control activities may restrict authorized users to the applications or functions commensurate with their assigned responsibilities, supporting an appropriate segregation of duties. Management designs other control activities to update access rights when employees change job functions or leave the entity. Management also designs control activities for access rights when different information technology elements are connected to each other.

Design Information Technology Acquisition, Development, and Maintenance

11.19 Management should design control activities over the acquisition, development, and maintenance of information technology.

11.20 Management designs control activities over the acquisition, development, and maintenance of information technology. Management may use the Systems Development Life Cycle (SDLC) framework in designing control activities. An SDLC provides a structure for a new information technology design by outlining specific phases and documenting requirements, approvals, and checkpoints within control activities over the acquisition, development, and maintenance of technology. Through the SDLC, management designs control activities over changes to technology. This may involve requiring authorization of change requests, reviewing the changes, approvals, testing results, and designing protocols to determine whether changes are made properly. Depending on the size and complexity of the entity, development of information technology and changes to the information technology may be included in one SDLC or two separate methodologies. Management evaluates the objectives and risks of the new technology in designing control activities over its SDLC.

11.21 Management may also acquire information technology through packaged software from vendors. Management incorporates into its information technology development methodologies for the acquisition of vendor packages and designs control activities over their selection, ongoing development, and maintenance. Control activities on the development, maintenance, and change of application software prevent unauthorized programs or modifications to existing programs.

11.22 Another alternative is outsourcing the development of information technology to service organizations. As for an SDLC developed internally, management designs control activities to meet objectives and address related risks. Management also evaluates the unique risks that utilizing a service organization presents for the completeness, accuracy, and validity of information submitted to and received from the service organization.

Principle 12 – Implement Control Activities

12.01 Management should implement control activities.

Attributes

12.02 The following attributes contribute to the design, implementation, and operating effectiveness of this principle:

a. Document Responsibilities through Policies - Management should document in policies the internal control responsibilities of the organization.

b. Perform Periodic Review - Management should periodically review the implementation of control activities to determine their continued relevance, redesign them when necessary, and communicate them as appropriate.

Document Responsibilities through Policies

12.03 Management should document in policies the internal control responsibilities of the organization.

12.04 Management documents in policies for each unit its responsibility for an operational process's objectives and related risks, control activity design, implementation, and operating effectiveness.[33] Each unit, with guidance from management, determines based on the objectives and related risks the number of policies necessary for the operational process. Each unit also documents policies in the appropriate level of detail to allow management to effectively monitor the control activity.

---

[33] See paras. 3.03 through 3.07 for further discussion of units.

> Elements of a written policy may include:
>
> • **Timeliness** – Management documents when a control activity and any follow-up corrective actions are performed.
>
> • **Corrective actions** – Management documents the need for appropriate follow-up when matters are identified that require investigation, and establishes responsibility for any corrective actions taken.
>
> • **Competence** – Management documents the level of competency required to perform a control activity. Requirements depend on factors such as the complexity of the control activity and the complexity and volume of the underlying transactions.

12.05 Those in key roles for the unit may further define policies through day-to-day procedures, depending on the rate of change in the operating environment and complexity of the operational process. Procedures may include the timing of when a control activity occurs, and any follow-up corrective actions to be performed by competent personnel if deficiencies are identified.[34] Management communicates to personnel the policies and procedures so that personnel can implement the control activities for their assigned responsibilities.

Perform Periodic Review

12.06 Management should periodically review the implementation of control activities to determine their continued relevance, redesign them when necessary, and communicate them as appropriate.

12.07 Management periodically reviews policies, procedures, and related control activities for continued relevance and effectiveness in achieving the entity's objectives or addressing related risks. If there is a significant change in an entity's process, management reviews this process in a timely manner after the change to ensure the control activities are designed and implemented appropriately. Changes may occur in personnel, operational processes, or information technology. Regulators, Congress, and OMB, may also change either an entity's objectives or how an entity is to achieve an objective. Management considers these changes in its periodic review.

---

[34] See paras. 17.09 through 17.10 for further discussion of corrective actions.

Information and Communication

Overview

Management uses quality information to support the internal control system. Effective information and communication is vital for an entity to run and control its operations. Entity management needs access to relevant and reliable communication related to internal as well as external events.

Principles

13. Management should use quality information.

14. Management should internally communicate the necessary quality information.

15. Management should externally communicate the necessary quality information.

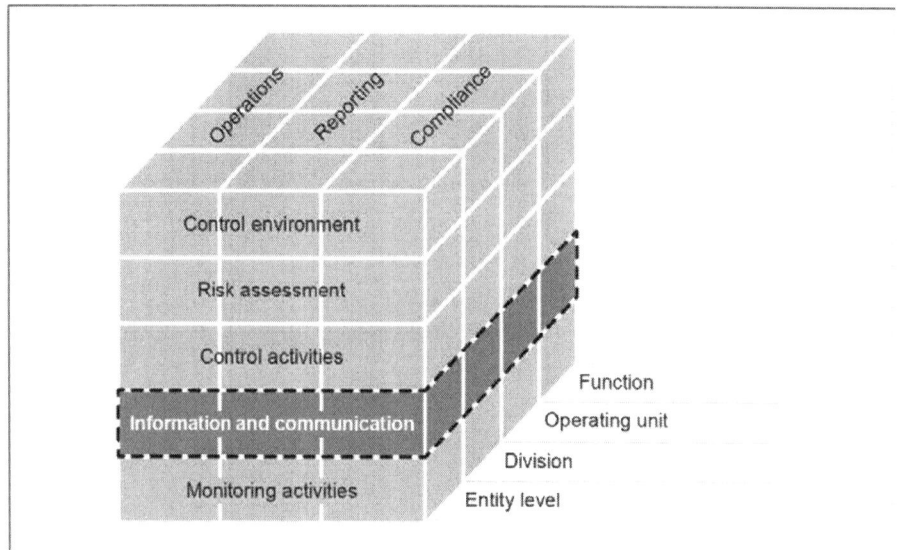

Source: COSO.

Principle 13 - Use Quality Information

13.01 Management should use quality information.

Attributes

13.02 The following attributes contribute to the design, implementation and operating effectiveness of this principle:

a. Identify Information Requirements - Management should design a process to identify information requirements.

b. Obtain Relevant Data from Reliable Sources - Management should obtain relevant data from reliable internal and external sources on a timely basis based on the identified information requirements.

c. Process Data into Quality Information - Management should process the obtained data into quality information.

Identify Information Requirements

13.03 Management should design a process to identify information requirements.

13.04 Management designs a process that uses the entity's objectives and related risks to identify the information requirements needed to achieve the objectives and address the risks. Information requirements consider the expectations of both internal and external users. Management defines the identified information requirements at the relevant level and requisite specificity for appropriate personnel.

13.05 Management identifies information requirements in an iterative and ongoing process that occurs throughout the performance of an effective internal control system. As change in the entity and its objectives and risks occur, management changes information requirements as needed to meet these modified objectives and address these modified risks.

Obtain Relevant Data from Reliable Sources

13.06 Management should obtain relevant data from reliable internal and external sources on a timely basis based on the identified information requirements.

13.07 Management obtains relevant data from reliable internal and external sources on a timely basis based on the identified information requirements. Relevant data has a logical connection with, or bearing upon, the identified information requirements. Reliable internal and external sources provide data that are reasonably free from error and bias and faithfully represent what they purport to represent. Management evaluates both internal and external sources of data to ensure that they are reliable. Sources of data can be operational, financial, or compliance related. Management obtains data on a timely basis to allow it to be used for effective monitoring.

Process Data into Quality Information

13.08 Management should process the obtained data into quality information.

13.09 Management processes the obtained data into quality information that supports the internal control system. This involves processing data into information and then evaluating the processed information to ensure that it is quality information. Quality information meets the identified information requirements by using relevant data from reliable sources. Quality information is appropriate, current, accurate, accessible, and provided on a timely basis. Management considers these characteristics as well as the information processing objectives in evaluating processed information and makes revisions when necessary to ensure that the information is quality information.[35] Management uses the quality information to make informed decisions and evaluate the entity's performance in achieving key objectives and addressing risks.

13.10 Management processes relevant data from reliable sources into quality information within the organization's information system. An information system is the people, processes, data, and technology

---

[35] See paras. 11.03 through 11.06 for further discussion of information processing objectives.

management organizes to obtain, communicate, or dispose of information.[36]

Principle 14 - Communicate Internally

14.01 Management should internally communicate the necessary quality information.

Attributes

14.02 The following attributes contribute to the design, implementation and operating effectiveness of this principle:

a. Communicate throughout the Entity - Management should communicate quality information throughout the entity utilizing established reporting lines.

b. Select Appropriate Method of Communication - Management should select appropriate methods to communicate internally.

Communicate throughout the Entity

14.03 Management should communicate quality information throughout the entity utilizing established reporting lines.

14.04 Management communicates quality information throughout the entity utilizing established reporting lines. Quality information is communicated down, across, up, and around reporting lines to all levels of the entity.

14.05 Management communicates quality information down and across reporting lines to enable personnel to perform key roles in achieving objectives, addressing risks, and supporting the internal control system. In these communications, management assigns the internal control responsibilities for key roles.

14.06 Management receives quality information about the entity's operational processes that flows up the reporting lines from personnel to help management achieve the entity's objectives.

---

[36] See paras. 11.03 through 11.06 for further discussion of information systems.

14.07 The oversight body receives quality information that flows up the reporting lines from management and personnel. Information relating to internal control communicated to the oversight body includes significant matters about the adherence to, changes in, or issues arising from the internal control system. This upward communication is necessary for the effective oversight of internal control.

14.08 Personnel utilize separate reporting lines to go around upward reporting lines when these lines are compromised. Laws and regulations may require entities to establish separate lines of communication, such as whistleblower and ethics hotlines, for communicating confidential information. Management informs employees of these separate reporting lines, how they operate, how they are to be used, and how the information will remain confidential.

Select Appropriate Methods of Communication

14.09 Management should select appropriate methods to communicate internally.

14.10 Management selects appropriate methods to communicate internally. Management considers a variety of factors in selecting an appropriate method of communication. Some factors to consider:

- Audience - The intended recipients of the communication

- Nature of Information - The purpose and type of information being communicated

- Availability - Information readily available to the audience when needed

- Cost - The resources used to communicate the information

- Legal or Regulatory requirements - Requirements by laws and regulations that may impact communication, such as retention requirements

14.11 Based on the consideration of the factors, management selects appropriate methods of communication, such as a written document, whether in hard copy or electronic format, or a face-to-face meeting. Management periodically evaluates the organization's methods of communication to ensure that the organization has the appropriate tools to communicate quality information throughout the entity on a timely basis.

Principle 15 - Communicate Externally

15.01 The organization should externally communicate the necessary quality information.

Attributes

15.02 The following attributes contribute to the design, implementation and operating effectiveness of this principle:

a. Communicate with External Parties - Management should communicate with, and obtain quality information from, external parties utilizing established reporting lines.

b. Select Appropriate Method of Communication - Management should select appropriate methods to communicate externally.

Communicate with External Parties

15.03 Management should communicate with, and obtain quality information from, external parties utilizing established reporting lines.

15.04 Management communicates with, and obtains quality information from, external parties utilizing established reporting lines. Open two-way external reporting lines allow for this communication. External parties include stakeholders,[37] suppliers, contractors, service organizations, regulators, external auditors, government entities, and the general public.

15.05 Management communicates quality information externally through reporting lines so that external parties can help the entity achieve its objectives and address related risks. Management includes in these communications information relating to the organization's events and activities that impact the internal control system.

15.06 Management receives information through reporting lines from external parties. Information communicated to management includes significant matters relating to risks, changes, or issues that impact the entity's internal control system. This communication is necessary for the effective operation of internal control. Management evaluates external

---

[37] See paras. 2.03 through 2.10 for further discussion of stakeholders.

GAO 13-830SP Green Book Exposure Draft

information received against the characteristics of quality information and information processing objectives and takes any necessary actions to ensure that the information is quality information.[38]

15.07 The oversight body receives information through reporting lines from external parties. Information communicated to the oversight body includes significant matters relating to risks, changes, or issues that impact the entity's internal control system. This communication is necessary for the effective oversight of internal control.

15.08 External parties utilize separate reporting lines when external reporting lines are compromised. Laws and regulations may require entities to establish separate lines of communication, such as whistleblower and ethics hotlines, for communicating confidential information. Management informs external parties of these separate reporting lines, how they operate, how they are to be used, and how the information will remain confidential.

Select Appropriate Methods of Communication

15.09 Management should select appropriate methods to communicate externally.

15.10 Management selects appropriate methods to communicate externally. Management considers a variety of factors in selecting an appropriate method of communication. Some factors to consider:

- Audience - The intended recipients of the communication

- Nature of Information - The purpose and type of information being communicated

- Availability - Information readily available to the audience when needed

- Cost - The resources used to communicate the information

- Legal or Regulatory requirements - Requirements by laws and regulations that may impact communication

---

[38] See paras. 11.03 through 11.06 for further discussion of information processing objectives.

15.11 Based on the consideration of the factors, management selects appropriate methods of communication, such as a written document, whether in paper or electronic format, or a face-to-face meeting. Management periodically evaluates the organization's methods of communication to ensure that the organization has the appropriate tools to communicate quality information throughout and outside of the entity on a timely basis.

15.12 In the federal government, organizations not only report to Congress and the President but to the general public as well. Organizations need to consider appropriate methods when communicating with such a broad audience.

Monitoring

Overview

Finally, since internal control is a dynamic process that has to be adapted continuously to the risks and changes an organization faces, monitoring of the internal control system is essential to help ensure that internal control remains aligned with changing objectives, environment, laws, resources, and risks. Internal control monitoring assesses the quality of performance over time and ensures that the findings of audits and other reviews are promptly resolved. Corrective actions are a necessary complement to control activities in order to achieve objectives.

Principles

16. Management should establish monitoring activities to monitor the internal control system and evaluate the results.

17. Management should ensure identified internal control deficiencies are remediated on a timely basis.

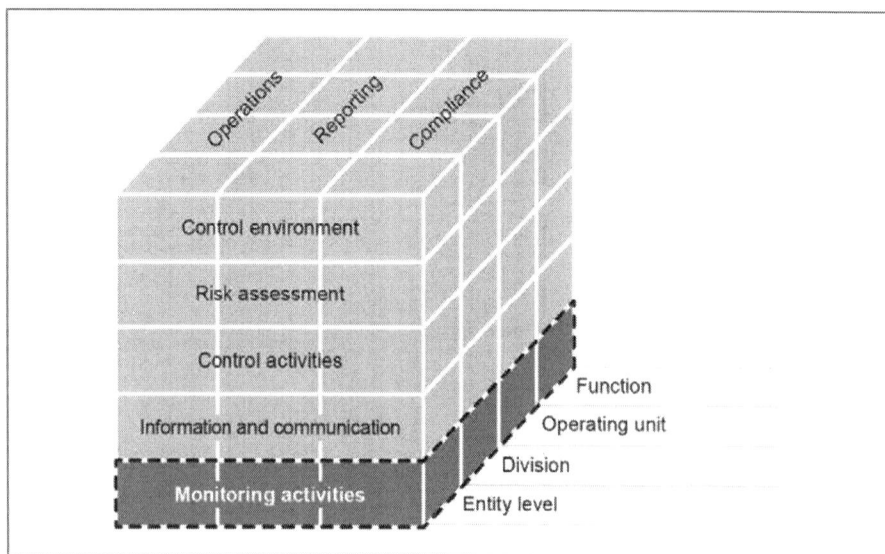

Source: COSO.

Principle 16 - Perform Monitoring Activities

16.01 Management should establish monitoring activities to monitor the internal control system and evaluate the results.

Attributes

16.02 The following attributes contribute to the design, implementation, and operating effectiveness of this principle:

a. Establish a Baseline - Management should establish a baseline for monitoring the internal control system.

b. Monitor Internal Control System - Management should monitor the internal control system through ongoing monitoring and separate evaluations.

c. Evaluate Results - Management should document and evaluate the results of ongoing monitoring and separate evaluations to identify internal control issues.

Establish a Baseline

16.03 Management should establish a baseline for monitoring the internal control system.

16.04 Management establishes a baseline to monitor the internal control system in supporting the entity in achieving its objectives. The baseline is the current state of the internal control system compared against management's design of the internal control system. The baseline represents the difference between the criteria of the design of the internal control system and condition of the internal control system at a specific point in time. In other words, the baseline consists of issues and deficiencies identified in an entity's internal control system.

16.05 Once established, management can use the baseline as criteria in evaluating the internal control system and make changes to reduce the difference between the criteria and condition. Management reduces this difference in one of two ways. Management either changes the design of the internal control system to better address the objectives and risks of the entity or improves the operating effectiveness of the internal control system. As part of monitoring, management determines when to revise the baseline to reflect changes in the internal control system.

Monitor Internal Control System

16.06 Management should monitor the internal control system through ongoing monitoring and separate evaluations.

16.07 Management monitors the internal control system through the monitoring activities of ongoing monitoring and separate evaluations. Ongoing monitoring is built into the entity's operations, performed continually, and responsive to change. Separate evaluations are used periodically and may provide feedback on the effectiveness of ongoing monitoring.

16.08 Management performs ongoing monitoring of the design and operating effectiveness of the internal control system as part of the normal course of operations. Ongoing monitoring includes regular management and supervisory activities, comparisons, reconciliations, and other routine actions. Ongoing monitoring may include automated tools, which can increase objectivity and efficiency by electronically evaluating controls and transactions.

16.09 Management uses separate evaluations to monitor the design and operating effectiveness of the internal control system at a specific time or of a specific function or process. The scope and frequency of separate evaluations depend primarily on the assessment of risks, effectiveness of ongoing monitoring, and rate of change within the entity and its environment. Separate evaluations may take the form of self-assessments, which include cross operating unit or cross functional evaluations.

16.10 Separate evaluations also include audits and other evaluations that may involve the review of control design and direct testing of internal control. These audits and other evaluations may be mandated by law and are performed by internal auditors, external auditors, the Inspectors General, and other external reviewers. Separate evaluations provide greater objectivity when performed by reviewers who do not have responsibility for the activities being evaluated.

16.11 Management retains responsibility for monitoring the effectiveness of internal control over the assigned processes performed by service organizations. Management uses ongoing monitoring, separate evaluations, or a combination of the two to obtain reasonable assurance over the operating effectiveness of the service organization's internal controls over the assigned process.[39] These monitoring activities related to service organizations may either be performed by management or performed by external parties and reviewed by management.

Evaluate Results

16.12 Management should evaluate and document the results of ongoing monitoring and separate evaluations to identify internal control issues.

16.13 Management evaluates and documents the results of ongoing monitoring and separate evaluations to identify issues in the internal control system. Management utilizes this evaluation to determine the effectiveness of the internal control system. Differences between the results of monitoring activities and the previously established baseline may indicate internal control issues, including undocumented changes in the internal control system or potential internal control deficiencies.

16.14 Management may identify changes in the internal control system that either have occurred or are needed due to changes in the entity and its environment. External parties can also help management identify issues in the internal control system. For example, complaints from the general public and regulator comments may indicate areas in the internal control system that need improvement. Management considers whether current controls address the identified issues and modifies controls if necessary.

Principle 17 – Remediate Deficiencies

17.01 Management should ensure identified internal control deficiencies are remediated on a timely basis.

---

[39] See the Overview: Service Organizations for further discussion of service organizations.

Attributes

17.02 The following attributes contribute to the design, implementation, and operating effectiveness of this principle:

a. Report Issues - Personnel should report internal control issues to appropriate internal and external parties on a timely basis.

b. Evaluate Issues - Management should evaluate and document internal control issues and determine appropriate corrective actions for internal control deficiencies on a timely basis.

c. Complete Corrective Actions - Management should complete and document corrective actions to remediate internal control deficiencies on a timely basis.

Report Issues

17.03 Personnel should report internal control issues to appropriate internal and external parties on a timely basis.

17.04 Personnel report internal control issues through established reporting lines to the appropriate internal and external parties on a timely basis to enable the entity to timely evaluate those issues.[40]

17.05 Personnel may identify internal control issues while performing their assigned internal control responsibilities. Personnel communicate these issues internally to the person in the key role responsible for the internal control or associated process and to at least one level of management above that individual. Depending on the nature of the issues, personnel may consider reporting certain issues to the oversight body. Such issues may include:

- Issues that cut across the organizational structure or extend outside the organization to service organizations, contractors, or suppliers.

- Issues that may not be remediated due to the interests of management, such as sensitive information regarding fraud or other illegal acts.[41]

---

[40] See paras. 14.03 through 14.08 for further discussion of internal reporting lines and paras. 15.03 through 15.08 for further discussion of external reporting lines.

[41] See paras. 8.03 through 8.05 for further discussion of fraud.

17.06 Depending on the entity's regulatory or compliance requirements, the entity may also be required to report issues externally to appropriate external parties, such as the legislators, regulators and standard-setting bodies that establish laws, rules, regulations, and standards to which the entity is subject.

Evaluate Issues

17.07 Management should evaluate and document internal control issues and determine appropriate corrective actions for internal control deficiencies on a timely basis.

17.08 Management evaluates and documents internal control issues and determines appropriate corrective actions for internal control deficiencies on a timely basis to ensure an effective internal control system. Management evaluates issues identified through monitoring activities or reported by personnel to determine whether any of the issues rise to the level of an internal control deficiency. Internal control deficiencies require further evaluation and remediation by management. An internal control deficiency can be in the design, implementation, or operating effectiveness of the internal control and its related process.[42] Management determines from the type of internal control deficiency the appropriate corrective actions to remediate the internal control deficiency on a timely basis. Management assigns responsibility and delegates authority to remediate the internal control deficiency.

Complete Corrective Actions

17.09 Management should complete and document corrective actions to remediate internal control deficiencies on a timely basis.

17.10 Management completes and documents corrective actions to remediate internal control deficiencies on a timely basis. Depending on the nature of the deficiency, either the oversight body or management oversees the prompt remediation of deficiencies by communicating the corrective actions to the appropriate level of the organizational structure and delegating authority for completing corrective actions to appropriate

---

[42] See the Overview: Evaluation of an Internal Control System for further discussion of evaluation of internal control deficiency.

personnel. Management, with oversight from the oversight body, tracks the status of remediation efforts to ensure that they are completed on a timely basis.

Glossary

The following terms are provided to assist in clarifying the *Standards for Internal Control in the Federal Government*. The most relevant paragraph numbers are provided for reference.

Terms

Application control activities - Controls that are incorporated directly into computer applications to help ensure the validity, completeness, accuracy, and confidentiality of transactions and data during application processing; application controls include controls over input, processing, output, master file, interface, and data management system controls (paragraph 11.10)

Application material - Additional information that provides further explanation of the principle and attribute requirements of internal control (Overview: Components, Principles and Attributes)

Baseline - The difference between the criteria of the design of the internal control system and condition of the internal control system at a specific point in time (paragraph 16.04)

Competence - The qualification to carry out assigned responsibilities (paragraph 4.04)

Complementary user entity controls - Controls that management of the service organization assumes, in the design of its service, will be implemented by user entities, and which, if necessary to achieve the control objectives stated in management's description of the service organization's system, are identified as such in that description (Overview: Service Organizations).

Contingency plans - The processes defined to address an organization's need to respond to sudden personnel changes impacting the organization (paragraph 4.10)

Control activities - The policies, procedures, techniques, and mechanisms that enforce management's directives to achieve the entity's objectives and address related risks (paragraph 10.04)

Deficiency - When the design, implementation, or operation of a control does not allow management or personnel, in the normal course of performing their assigned functions, to achieve control objectives and address related risks (Overview: Evaluation of Deficiencies in Internal Control)

Detective control - An activity that is designed to discover when an entity is not achieving an objective or addressing a risk before the entity's operation has concluded and corrects the actions so that the entity achieves the objective or addresses the risk (paragraph 10.07)

Entity-level control - Controls that have a pervasive effect on an organization's internal control system; entity-level controls may include controls related to the entity's risk assessment process, control environment, service organizations, management override, monitoring, and year-end financial reporting (paragraph 10.12)

Fraud - Involves obtaining something of value through willful misrepresentation (paragraph 8.04)

General control activities - The policies and procedures that apply to all or a large segment of an entity's information systems; general controls include security management, logical and physical access, configuration management, segregation of duties, and contingency planning (paragraph 11.09)

Green Book - The commonly used name for the *Standards for Internal Control in the Federal Government* (Overview: Foreword)

Information system - The people, processes, data, and technology management organizes to obtain, communicate, or dispose of information (paragraph 11.04)

Information technology - Technology-enabled information processes (paragraph 11.04)

Inherent risk - The risk to an entity in the absence of management's response to the risk (paragraph 7.05)

Internal control - The plans, methods, policies, and procedures used to fulfill the mission, strategic plan, goals, and objectives of the organization (Overview: Definition of Internal Control)

Internal control system - A continuous built-in component of operations, effected by people, that provides reasonable assurance, not absolute assurance, that an organization's objectives will be achieved (Overview: An Internal Control System)

Key role - A position in an organizational structure that is assigned an overall responsibility of an entity (paragraph 3.09)

Likelihood of occurrence - The possibility that a risk will occur (paragraph 7.09)

Magnitude of impact - Magnitude of deficiency that could result from the risk and is affected by factors such as the size, pace, and duration of the risk's impact (paragraph 7.09)

Management - Entity personnel who are directly responsible for all activities of an organization, including the design, implementation, and operating effectiveness of an entity's internal control system (Overview: Roles in an Internal Control System)

Organizational structure - The operating units, operational processes, and other structures management uses to achieve objectives (Overview: Internal Control and the Entity)

Oversight body - Those responsible for overseeing management's design, implementation, and operation of an internal control system (Overview: Roles in an Internal Control System)

Performance measure - A means of evaluating the entity's performance in achieving objectives (paragraph 6.09)

Policies - Statements of responsibility for an operational process's objectives and related risks, control activity design, implementation, and operating effectiveness (paragraph 12.04)

Preventive control - An activity that is designed to prevent an entity from failing to achieve an objective or addressing a risk (paragraph 10.07)

Qualitative objectives - Subjective objectives where management may need to design performance measures that indicate a level or degree of performance, such as milestones (paragraph 6.09)

Quality information - Information from relevant and reliable data that is appropriate, current, accurate, accessible, provided on a timely basis, and meets the need of identified information requirements (paragraph 13.09)

Quantitative objectives - Calculable objectives where performance measures may be a targeted percentage or numerical value (paragraph 6.09)

Reasonable assurance - A high degree of confidence, but not absolute confidence (Overview: An Internal Control System)

Reporting lines - Communication lines at all levels of the organization that provide methods of communication that can flow down, across, up, and around the organizational structure (paragraph 3.06)

Residual risk - The risk that remains after management's response to inherent risk (paragraph 7.05)

Risk - The possibility that an event will occur and adversely affect the achievement of objectives (paragraph 7.03)

Risk tolerance - The acceptable level of variation in performance relative to the achievement of objectives (paragraph 6.11)

Security management - The information processes and control activities related to access rights in an entity's information technology (paragraph 11.16)

Segregation of duties - The separation of the authority, custody and accounting of an operation (paragraph 10.17)

Service organization - An external party that performs operational process(es) for an entity (Overview: Service Organizations)

Succession plans - The processes that address an organization's need to replace competent personnel over the long term (paragraph 4.10)

Transaction control activities - Actions built directly into operational processes to support the organization in achieving its objectives and addressing related risks (paragraph 10.13)

Appendix I – Comptroller General's Advisory Council on Standards for Internal Control in the Federal Government and GAO Project Team

Advisory Council Members (2013-2015)

Jon Rymer, Chair
Federal Deposit Insurance Corporation

Brett Baker
National Science Foundation

Lisa Casias
Department of Commerce

Carole Clay
State Department

Melinda DeCorte
Cotton & Company LLP

Stephen Eells
New Jersey, Office of the State Auditor

Carol M. Eyermann
National Science Foundation

William (Bill) Hughes
MorganFranklin

Scot Janssen
KPMG LLP

John Kaschak
Pennsylvania Office of the Budget, Bureau of Audits

David L. Landsittel
COSO

Samuel T. Mok
Condor International Advisors, LLC

Kenneth J. Mory
City of Austin, Texas

Dan Murrin
Ernst & Young

Annette K. Pridgen
Jackson State University

Sandra B. Richtermeyer
Xavier University

Neil Ryder
Department of Justice

Peggy Sherry
Department of Homeland Security

F. Michael Taylor
Hanover County Government

David A. Von Moll
Commonwealth of Virginia Office of the State Comptroller

David M. Zavada
Kearney & Company

GAO Project Team

Steven J. Sebastian, Managing Director
James R. Dalkin, Project Director
Robert F. Dacey, Chief Accountant
Heather I. Keister, Assistant Director
Kristen A. Kociolek, Assistant Director
Brian S. Harechmak, Senior Auditor
Bernice M. Lemaire, Senior Auditor
Mary O. Osorno, Senior Auditor
Christie A. Pugnetti, Senior Auditor
Grant L. Simmons, Senior Auditor
Doris G. Yanger, Senior Auditor
Lee Evans, Auditor
Marci L. Goasdone, Auditor
Debra L. Hoffman, Auditor
Alan S. MacMullin, Auditor
Andrew D. Seehusen, Auditor
Jacquelyn Hamilton, Deputy Assistant General Counsel
Francine M. DelVecchio, Supervisory Communications Analyst

Printed in Great Britain
by Amazon.co.uk, Ltd.,
Marston Gate.